Contents

Introduction — 4

Section I: Supporting independent Black candidates

Newark SWP Supports CIO, Negro Candidates — 5
by George Breitman

Newark Negro Community Fights for Representation — 7
by George Breitman

Newark Elects First Negro to City Council — 9
by Daniel Roberts

Should Negroes Stick to Democratic Party? — 10
by Fred Hart (George Breitman)

Section II: What is independent political action?

Fundamental Aspects of the Atkinson Question — 13
by Farrell Dobbs

Appendix: Comments on the Trotsky-Johnson Discussion — 19
by George Breitman

Section III: The Freedom Now Party

Freedom Now — 22
Excerpt from Resolution of Socialist Workers Party

Manifesto Issued in Capital for Freedom Now Party — 23
by Leslie Evans

A Call for a Freedom Now Party for 1964 — 24

In Defense of Move for Freedom Now Party — 25
by LaMar Barron

FNP Files for Place on Michigan Ballot — 27
by George Breitman

Detroit SWP Candidate Withdraws in Favor of Freedom Now Nominee — 29

The FNP Platform — 29

What the Freedom Now Party Has Accomplished 31
by George Breitman

Further Discussion on Freedom Now Party 35
by George Breitman

Section IV: The Lowndes County Freedom Organization

The Black Panther Party: A Report from
Lowndes County 38
by John Benson

How the Black Panther Party Was Organized 42
by John Hullet

What I Saw in Lowndes County, Alabama 46
by Elizabeth Barnes

Black Power and the Democrats 48
by Barry Sheppard

Section V: The case for an independent Black party

Resolution of the Socialist Workers Party 52

Section VI: Two campaigns by Carl Stokes

Cleveland Negro Almost Upset Machine 64
by Eric Reinthaler

Why President Johnson Favors Stokes for Cleveland Mayor 66
by Eric Reinthaler

Stokes' Cleveland Victory 67
by Elizabeth Barnes

Stokes-Hatcher Victory: A Real Gain for Blacks? 68
by Elizabeth Barnes

Section VII: The Black Panther Party

The Black Panther Party Platform and Program 71

Seattle Black Panther Party to Run Two
Candidates for State Assembly 72
by Debbie Leonard and Will Reissner

The Panther–Peace and Freedom Alliance 74
by Derrick Morrison

Retreat from a Strategy of Mass Action — 76
by Derrick Morrison

Why Did the Black Panther Party Split? — 78
by Tony Thomas

Seale-Brown Campaign Steers Oakland Blacks Toward Democratic Party Swamp — 82
by Rick Congress

Section VIII: The Gary Convention

The Gary Convention and the Struggle for a Black Party — 84
by Derrick Morrison

Preamble to the National Black Political Agenda — 88

The Meaning of the Black Political Agenda — 90
by Tony Thomas

Section IX: After Gary

From Gary To Miami — 97
by Derrick Morrison

Need for Independent Party Raised at National Black Political Convention — 98
by Norman Oliver

Black Power: How It Will Be Won — 101
by Tony Thomas

Black Convention Debates Electoral Action — 105
by Baxter Smith

Working-class Politics and Capitalist Politics — 107
by Jack Barnes

Introduction

The following selection of articles and documents from the *Militant* newspaper and from other publications of the socialist movement dealing with the question of independent Black political action, is a record of some of the major developments in the struggle for independent working-class political action from 1954 up to the formation of the National Black Independent Political Party, which was founded in November 1980. (This bulletin ends before this latter development; for information on the NBIPP see the companion bulletin, *The National Black Independent Political Party: An Important Step Forward for Blacks and Other American Workers* (Pathfinder Press, 1982).)

There is greater interest today in independent working-class political action than at any time since the 1940s. This new interest is being sparked by the government's austerity and take-back campaign domestically and by the escalating war drive internationally on the part of both the Democratic and Republican parties. More and more workers—Black, white, and Latino—are coming to understand that these anti-working-class and racist policies are a bipartisan effort of both capitalist parties; that the Democrats and Republicans offer no other solution to the crisis of world capitalism except austerity and war.

In this framework the thinking of a growing number of working people tends to move toward the conclusion that an independent working-class political alternative is the only realistic perspective for the defense of their basic interests.

An important reflection of this tendency has been the discussion taking place in the press of some of the major unions during the past few years about whether labor should organize its own party. The discussion on independent political action is also a prominent feature in the Black press, such as the *Amsterdam News* in New York, the largest-circulating Black newspaper in the country.

Most of the attempts at independent working-class political action in the last several decades have taken place in the Black movement—reflecting the response both of exploited workers and of an oppressed nationality fighting for its liberation. Most of the questions raised today around this question, including around the question of independent Black political action, are similar to those discussed and debated out over the last twenty-five years.

Therefore, we feel the selections in this bulletin will prove helpful for activists in the Black and labor movements who are attempting to chart a correct course today.

This bulletin is not meant to be a comprehensive history of the struggle for independent Black political action, much less of the Black movement as a whole. It is a collection of contemporary articles and documents covering some of the most important chapters in the Black movement's experiences with independent political action, and which trace the development of the Socialist Workers Party's perspectives on this question.

The bulletin is broken down into nine sections. Each one is prefaced with a brief note that explains some of the background to the section's contents. Most of the articles have been reproduced from the original source, so all typographical errors appear as they did in the original.

Mac Warren
Malik Miah
JUNE 1982

SECTION I
SUPPORTING INDEPENDENT BLACK CANDIDATES

The Socialist Workers Party has supported Black candidates who ran independently of and in opposition to the Democratic and Republican parties ever since the 1940s. One example of such a candidacy occurred in 1954 in the municipal elections in Newark, New Jersey, an election that featured independent labor, as well as independent Black, candidates.

This section includes several articles by George Breitman and Daniel Roberts from the *Militant* about this particular campaign. Breitman was the Socialist Workers Party's candidate for U.S. Senate in New Jersey in 1954. In addition, we are reprinting a 1954 *Militant* article, "Should Negroes Stick to Democratic Party?" which is a reply to the Communist Party's perspective of diverting the Black struggle back into the Democratic Party whenever Blacks attempt to break out of the two-party framework.

Newark SWP Supports CIO, Negro Candidates
by George Breitman

NEWARK, April 27—The Socialist Workers Party today announced support of four candidates for the Newark City Council in the election to be held May 11. Two of these are CIO candidates, and two are representatives of the Negro community.

The elections are the first to be held under the new Mayor-Council form of government approved in a referendum last November to replace the City Commission form. As was predicted by the SWP last year, the change-over from one form to another has shaken up the local political picture and encouraged the emergence of new political currents and alignments.

The most significant was the decision of the Essex-West Hudson CIO Council to run two CIO leaders for the City Council. They are James T. Callaghan, organization director of District 4, IUE-CIO, running for councilman-at-large; and Jerry Leopaldi, president of the big Federal Local 447, IUE-CIO, running for councilman in the East Ward.

This is not the first time the CIO has endorsed CIO members running for office, usually on the Democratic ticket. What is new in the present situation is that the CIO has *sponsored* Callaghan and Leopaldi and has assumed the major responsibility for financing and running their campaigns.

Against democrat slate

Municipal elections here are supposed to be "nonpartisan"—that is, no regular party label appears on the ballot. But this is a mere technicality, and the Democratic machine gets around it by drawing up its own informal slate and then passing down the word to its wardheelers to support that slate and oppose all others.

The significant thing about the Callaghan-Leopaldi candidacies is that they are not included on the Democratic machine's slate for the Council. In fact, the Democratic county boss approached Callaghan and asked him to take a place on his

Reprinted from the *Militant*, May 3, 1954

slate. Although CIO candidates generally have accepted such offers in the past, Callaghan turned it down this time.

Thus Callaghan and Leopaldi are running as independent candidates, sponsored by the CIO, and opposed by the corrupt Democratic machine and its candidates.

Their election under these circumstances would be a blow against capitalist politics. It would prove that labor can elect its own candidates. It would strengthen the movement for an independent Labor Party by showing that such a party can win office under its own steam. That is why the Socialist Workers Party favors their election.

One of Newark's biggest scandals is the fact that the Negro people represent over one-sixth of the population but have never had any top-level representation in the city government. The Socialist Workers Party urges the voters of Newark to correct this situation by electing Negro councilmen on May 11.

Harry Hazelwood Jr., former president of the local branch of the National Association for the Advancement of Colored People, has the support of the whole Negro community in his campaign for councilman-at-large. The SWP advocates his election.

It is unfortunate that in the Central Ward there are three Negro candidates, rather than a single candidate supported by the entire Negro community in that ward. This split endangers the chances of electing a Negro councilman. Irvine I. Turner is the candidate in the Central Ward who is most representative of the Negro community and has the greatest support among its working people. For this reason the SWP advocates his election and urges the Central Ward voters to unite behind his candidacy.

Negro representation in office is not only the right of Negroes but a necessity for white workers. The election of Negro councilmen who would be responsible to the Negro community will benefit labor too, because labor and the Negro people have common problems and common aspirations. In their own interest, the whole labor movement and all white workers should vote for Hazelwood and Turner.

While supporting these four candidates, we must point out that their programs do not go far enough, and that they still have not made a political break with the two-party system even though they are running against the candidates of the old parties. This weakens and limits the effectiveness of their campaigns.

Callaghan and Leopaldi, for example, call for more low-rent housing in Newark. This is good and necessary. But the truth is that Newark by itself cannot provide the money for an adequate housing and slum-clearance program. The truth is also that such a housing program (along with other progressive legislation) is blocked in Washington by both the Democrats and Republicans and their huge expenditures for war preparations.

Labor candidates in the Newark elections ought to state these facts openly. While running for office in Newark, they ought to expose the capitalist politicians in both old parties in Washington who prevent decent housing in Newark. And they ought to draw the necessary conclusion that now is the time to form a national as well as local Labor Party to take power and solve the housing and other problems.

Citizens committee

Another weakness of the Callaghan-Leopaldi campaigns is that they have, up to this point, put too much reliance on the help they hope to get from the Newark Citizens Committee on Municipal Government, and not enough emphasis on the fact that they are labor candidates.

The Citizens Committee is a non-partisan coalition formed last year to conduct the fight for adoption of the Mayor-Council form of government. Originally it included the CIO, AFL, Chamber of Commerce, Americans for Democratic Action and other local organizations. It follows a general ADA line.

After winning last November's referendum, the Citizens Committee decided to go into politics in the May 11 election, becoming in effect the nucleus of a local third party reform movement. At this point the Chamber of Commerce withdrew from the committee. The only mass strength left in the committee was the AFL and CIO.

Last month the Citizens Committee endorsed the Democratic incumbent for mayor, a slate for the four councilmen-at-large seats (including Callaghan, Hazelwood, a teacher and a lawyer advertised as speaking for the viewpoint of "business"), and recommended a number of candidates for councilmen in the five wards (including Leopaldi, but not Turner).

In order to get the Citizens Committee endorsements for themselves, Callaghan and Leopaldi committed themselves (with the CIO's permission) to support of the committee's full slate. But the CIO, to its credit, has taken a stand at least partially independent of the Citizens Committee, while remaining affiliated to it.

Last night the CIO Council rejected the Citizens Committee's candidate for mayor, voting not to endorse anyone for that post. It also rejected the Citizens Committee's "business" candidate, endorsing instead a CIO member who is running on his own initiative, without CIO sponsorship. In the Central Ward it voted to endorse Turner, in opposition to the man backed by the Citizens Committee. And it endorsed Hazelwood.

After the Citizens Committee's slate was picked, the AFL Essex Trades Council withdrew from the committee and endorsed some of the candidates on the regular Democratic slate. This left the Citizens Committee with only one strong affiliate, the CIO, and the CIO is spending its money on its own candidates.

Thus the Citizens Committee has not been able to make much of an impact in this election. Although the members of its slate are supposed to be campaigning jointly, the truth is that all of them, including the CIO candidates, "have been campaigning strictly on their own," as the April 17 Newark News put it.

While getting little help from the Citizens Committee, Callaghan and Leopaldi are trying to make themselves "more palatable" to non-labor voters by minimizing and relegating to the background the fact that they are CIO candidates, by placing great stress on their Citizens Committee endorsements, etc.

This is a serious mistake. Some CIO leaders think it is "sectarian" to make their CIO sponsorship the main axis of the Callaghan-Leopaldi campaigns; but this idea is all wet. Whatever they may say or do, Callaghan and Leopaldi are viewed by the public and the press primarily and above all as CIO candidates, and they will win or lose on that basis. They won't get more votes by acting half-ashamed about their CIO sponsorship, but they may lose some. Their success will depend on how much they can inspire the rank and file workers, AFL as well as CIO, with the idea that their candidacies represent something new, clean and independent in politics.

A step forward

Despite these shortcomings, we favor the election of Callaghan and Leopaldi as a step away from the two-party system and toward an independent Labor Party. And despite the inadequacies in the programs of Hazelwood and Turner, we favor their election because it would correct an injustice to the Negro people and because they too are opposed by the old party machines.

The election of these candidates would be a blow against the two-party system and an encouraging move toward the formation of an independent Labor Party based on the unions, the Negro people, housewives, youth, working farmers and the lower middle class.

A Labor Party, equipped with a militant program, could run its own candidates for office in Newark, in Trenton and in Washington, kick the Republicans and Democrats out of power, and begin to solve the problems of war, unemployment, McCarthyism, Jim Crow, Taft-Hartleyism, high prices, high taxes, high profits and general insecurity.

Newark Negro Community Fights for Representation
by George Breitman

NEWARK, May 4—The Newark Negro community's growing unity, militancy and determination to elect Negro candidates to the City Council are the most encouraging development in the final stages of the current municipal election campaign.

The elections will be held May 11. Four

Reprinted from the *Militant*, May 10, 1954

councilmen-at-large are to be elected by the city as a whole, and five councilmen are to be elected by the voters in the five wards. If no candidate gets a majority, there will be runoffs on June 15 between the top eight at-large candidates, and between the top two in each of the wards.

The Socialist Workers Party is supporting James T. Callaghan (at-large) and Jerry Leopaldi (East Ward) because they are CIO-sponsored candidates running independently of the old party machines, and Harry Hazelwood (at-large) and Irvine Turner (Central Ward) because they are independent Negro candidates reflecting the demand of the Negro community for top-level representation in the city government.

Hazelwood, former president of the NAACP branch here, is the only Negro at-large candidate and won the immediate and more or less complete support of the Negro community. But the situation in the Central Ward was more complicated—and more dynamic.

Most of the city's Negro population lives in the Central Ward, but in the ward itself Negroes represent only 51%. Efforts were made to unite all Negro organizations in the ward around a single candidacy, but these fell through because of factionalism, petty personal ambitions, etc. Three Negro candidates filed—Irvine Turner, former newspaperman; Roger Yancey, former U.S. assistant district attorney; and Samuel Stewart, school attendance officer.

Yancey was the choice of the Negro "talented tenth"—the NAACP and Urban League leadership, the local Afro-American, the middle class professionals. These people were contemptuous of and hostile to Turner on the ground that he was too "nationalistic," didn't have a college diploma, etc.

Yancey also received the recommendation of the liberal Newark Citizens Committee, a loose coalition aiming at civic reform and possibly a local third party. But there was one thing Yancey didn't have and that Turner did have—and that was the support of the rank and file Negroes in the Central Ward.

Turner had this support because he had a principle—the right of Negro representation in office. Yancey hemmed and hawed and said, "I don't want you to vote for me because I am a Negro and I don't want you to vote against me for the same reason." Fearing to lose the support of white voters by stressing the principle of Negro representation, he had nothing to offer that could arouse the rank and file Negroes. And he didn't win any white support in the ward thereby either.

Turner, on the other hand, was forthright and aggressive. He told everyone—white and Negro—that the Negro community had the right to representation, and that that was what he was campaigning for. This created enthusiasm among Negroes and respect among white people in the ward who are sympathetic to the Negro struggle for equality.

The struggle came to a head last week when the CIO Council made its endorsements. Originally the CIO leaders were under pressure from the Citizens Committee, with which the CIO is affiliated, to endorse Yancey. The Afro-American also applied such pressure on the CIO, even stooping to red-baiting Turner because he accepts the support of the Negro Labor Council.

But the pro-Turner sentiment in the ward became too clear and too strong to be ignored. The Baptist Ministers Conference and the Modern Beauticians, among many other organizations, came out for Turner. The CIO members in the ward let their leaders know that they favored Turner overwhelmingly, and that the CIO's own candidates would suffer among Negro voters if the CIO backed Yancey. And so the CIO Council, to its credit, rejected the pressure of the Citizens Committee and the talented tenth and endorsed Turner.

That settled it. Two days later Yancey announced his withdrawal from the race and began proceedings to try to get his name blocked off the ballot. In a fairly good statement he urged Turner and Stewart to get together and agree to have one of them withdraw. The pressure is now on Stewart to follow Yancey's example.

Whether or not Stewart will do this, and whether or not Yancey's name will be removed from the ballot, the fact is that practical unity in the Negro community has already been achieved behind the Turner candidacy. This reflects both the power of the demand for Negro representation, and the influence that the labor movement, and especially the CIO, wields in the Negro community.

The CIO's endorsement not only enabled the

Turner forces to take the unchallenged leadership of the Negro community in this election, it also opened the door for them to white workers in the CIO unions. If, as seems likely, Turner faces a white candidate in the runoffs, this factor can prove to be decisive.

Turner is already making full use of this opportunity. While continuing to mobilize Negro voters, he is appealing to white workers and the labor movement too. His latest poster records his CIO support in the same large-sized type as is used for his own name.

CIO weaknesses

This is in contrast to the posters and general literature of the CIO-sponsored candidates, Callaghan and Leopaldi. They subordinate their CIO sponsorship, almost as if they were frightened by their own boldness in running independently of the old machines. This weakens their appeal considerably because it makes it harder for them to be distinguished from run-of-the-mill candidates.

It also is responsible for their failure so far to generate the enthusiasm and broad rank and file participation that have become such a notable feature of the Turner campaign. It is fortunate for them that, despite their own reticence, they are known publicly only as the CIO's candidates; otherwise they wouldn't have a chance of reaching the runoffs. But it is a fact that their chances of being elected have been put in jeopardy by the way in which they are campaigning.

Despite these faults, the Socialist Workers Party is working for the election of Callaghan and Leopaldi as well as Turner and Hazelwood. Their election would stimulate further independent labor and Negro campaigns and the general movement for a Labor Party here and elsewhere.

Newark Elects First Negro to City Council
by Daniel Roberts

NEWARK, June 16—The Negro community of Newark scored an encouraging victory yesterday when it elected Irvine I. Turner to the City Council from the Central Ward. Turner is the first Negro ever to be elected to the Newark city government.

He ran as an independent in the non-partisan elections and campaigned vigorously on the issue of the right of Negro representation.

In addition, the Newark voters elected James T. Callaghan, councilmanic candidate at large sponsored by the CIO. Harry Hazelwood Jr., another independent Negro candidate running at-large, while defeated, received the highest city-wide vote that a Negro candidate ever polled.

Turner obtained 7,637 votes against 5,736 cast for his white opponent, John Salvato, or 57% of the total. The Negro community comprises 51% of the population in the ward. These figures indicate that the colored candidate was able to unite the Negro vote behind him and get it out solidly to the polls. He was able to win considerable white backing besides.

The election in Central Ward was hotly contested. Salvato, a Democratic wardheeler who had the backing of the Democratic party, sought to inflame anti-Negro sentiment. His racist appeals were presented under the slogan "Prevent Racial Discrimination," but he made it clear that what he meant was "Prevent 'discrimination' against whites by voting white."

His cards with this slogan were circulated primarily in the white districts. One of them featured the slogan on one side and separate photographs of Salvato and Turner on the other with the subcaption "Vote for One—But Vote!" The only purpose that Salvato had for printing his opponent's picture was to contrast the white to the Negro candidate in an appeal to prejudice.

In another folder, Salvato redbaited Turner. This type of attack stems from Turner's readiness to accept support from the Negro Labor Council,

Reprinted from the *Militant*, June 21, 1954

whose active campaigning played a large part in his election, and from Turner's refusal to issue anti-Communist declarations in general. But neither Salvato's reactionary appeals nor the sizeable funds at his disposal could shake the unity and militancy of the Negro community. These were the key to Turner's success.

Callaghan's election, unlike Turner's was not a clear-cut victory for principle. Callaghan hid the fact throughout the campaign that he was an independent candidate of the CIO. He didn't stand out in the race or inspire great enthusiasm. For this reason he again polled a low vote in the Central Ward, where, because of its Negro majority he should have received his greatest backing. The fault for Callaghan's unprincipled race was partly his and partly that of the CIO leadership. The contradiction between the CIO's original intention to elect a labor councilman and the shabby way in which it followed through was glaringly revealed by a letter sent out by the Essex-West Hudson CIO Council to all its Newark members on June 9.

This letter makes a correct analogy between the political arena and the factory. It says, "Remember, you wouldn't vote for a boss to become your shop steward. Then why vote to make a boss your city councilman?"

All this is true. But then why didn't the CIO sponsor a full slate of "stewards" for the Council instead of running Callaghan alone? Why did the CIO slate include political representatives of the bosses in the form of Democratic and Republican politicians? Why did the CIO virtually confine its campaign activities on behalf of Callaghan to this letter instead of mobilizing all its forces behind him?

As it turned out, Callaghan, although running independently, owes his election in good part to the support he accepted from Mayor Carlin and the Democrats. This recourse to aid from management's political representatives—denounced in the CIO's letter—ties Callaghan to the Democratic party and weakens his role of "shop steward" which the CIO intended he should play on the Council.

Hazelwood ran last of the eight at-large candidates, but registered a gain of 5,000 votes over his total in the May 11 primaries. He had united Negro backing but it was the failure of the labor movement to actively campaign for him, despite the CIO's endorsement, that was the biggest factor in Hazelwood's defeat.

Should Negroes Stick to Democratic Party?
by Fred Hart (George Breitman)

At the end of World War II the leadership of the Communist Party launched a great hue and cry against the policy of class collaboration and revisionism which they had been following for the previous four years and which they gave the convenient name of "Browderism." Browder was made the sole scapegoat for this policy and expelled from the party. The Stalinists began to denounce the Democratic Party, helped to form the Progressive Party and swore that never again would they commit the "mistake" of supporting capitalist parties or the policy of the capitalist lesser evil.

Now it's 1954, and the Stalinists have published a draft program, "The American Way to Jobs, Peace and Democracy," which brings them full circle and all the way back to—"Browderism."

The crassly class-collaborationist character of the CP program has been exposed in previous issues of the Militant (March 15, March 29, May 3, May 10). Here we want to deal only with the perspective that the Stalinists today hold out for the Negro struggle.

Democrats' role
The Democratic Party is traditionally the party of white supremacy. Its Northern wing spouts fine talk about FEPC (to woo the Northern Negro and labor vote) but its Southern wing (Dixiecrats and

Reprinted from the *Militant*, June 14, 1954

non-Dixiecrats alike) always vetoes FEPC and other anti-Jim Crow legislation. There is a division of labor between the two wings, and when Northern workers and Negroes help to put the Democrats in power nationally, they thereby give the Southern Democrats, by virtue of their greater seniority, the chairmanships of congressional committees and enable them all the more effectively to block all progressive legislation.

Yet it is this Democratic Party that the Stalinists today, as in the days of Browder, are urging and pleading the Negro people to elect and put in office.

The next big step the Negro movement must take in order to exert its political influence against the Jim Crow system is to break with the Democratic Party.

Yet that is what the Stalinists fear and want to prevent at all costs.

Perry's fears
One has only to read the article by the Stalinist leader, Pettis Perry, discussing the CP's draft program in the May Political Affairs, to see how determined they are to keep the Negro movement trapped on the Democratic merry-go-round.

The Democrats had better wise up and get on the ball, Perry says; and if they don't know what's good for them, he's ready to advise them.

Take the movement for Negro representation in office, which is growing and spreading. The Democrats are not "coming forward positively on this issue," they are "hedging," he complains. While the Republicans have Negro candidates for Congress in Philadelphia and Baltimore, the Democrats have only one new Negro candidate for Congress in Cleveland. The Republicans are doing this in order to "embarrass the Democratic Party," and Perry is worried; he wants the Democrats to avoid embarrassment by running more Negro candidates themselves.

It's not only the Democrats Perry is concerned about however: "For, if the situation continues as it is, sooner or later the Negro people will put the question: What is the value of the political alliance with the Democratic Party...?"

The question
That of course would be a terrible question—for the Democrats, and anyone else who wants to keep the Negroes tied to the Democrats. But it's a logical question for anyone who is concerned with advancing the political struggle against Jim Crow, whose chief buttress is the Democratic Party. The question is not only logical but inevitable, and the sooner it is asked and answered, the sooner the Negro people will be able to make genuine progress.

"Unfortunately," Perry continues gloomily, "when this question is raised, some people, including our own, ask the question: How would it be possible for the Negro people to desert such an alliance? Where would they go? Obviously the answer to that question is that it is possible that in the midst of such a situation the Negro people may decide to go it alone. This, in our judgment, would be wrong...."

That's why the Stalinists are begging the Democrats to get a new and less embarrassing look. That's why they are exerting all the influence they have to pervert and channelize back into the Democratic Party the current promising developments toward independent political action among Negroes, today taking the form primarily of movements for Negro representation in office.

And that's why militant Negroes have to fight the Stalinists as well as the capitalist politicians if they want to raise the Negro struggle for equality to a higher political level and to equip it with a program and a perspective capable of bringing victory.

Why the worry
The Stalinists profess horror at the prospect of Negroes "going it alone"—that is, breaking with the old parties—because it conflicts with the Kremlin's aim of seeking a deal with U.S. capitalism by penetrating the Democratic Party. But militant Negroes have no reason whatever to be frightened by such a prospect.

What the Negro people need is a political alliance with the labor movement to form a new party, a Labor Party. The main obstacle to such a party is not the Negro people but the labor leaders, who continue to drag along behind the Democrats.

The question is: Must the Negroes mark time patiently until the labor leaders eventually get pushed off their seats and into motion for a Labor

Party? Or can Negroes even now take independent action to hasten the Labor Party development?

Must Negroes Wait?

The Stalinists say the Negro movement must wait. That's because of the Kremlin's diplomatic aims. But it's also because they have no confidence in the independent role of the Negro movement, because they don't believe that Negroes by themselves are capable of leading or decisively affecting political developments.

Our view is altogether different. A minority group like the Negroes cannot abolish the Jim Crow system by itself, but it can hasten its abolition, and win the necessary allies to assure its abolition, by following a bold, militant and independent policy of struggle. That's what happened in the fight against slavery. And that's what can happen in the fight for a Labor Party.

As we pointed out in this paper last Feb. 8, a break of the Negro people with the Democratic Party would have thoroughly progressive consequences. For one thing, it would put heavy pressure on the labor leaders "who know how difficult it would be for them to help elect their Democratic candidates without the support of the Negro voters. If the labor leaders can be shown that the Negro people are no longer going to vote Democrat and that as a result the Democrats will stand little chance of being elected, then the result would be to weaken the alliance between the labor leaders and the Democrats and to force the labor movement into at least considering a new political policy. This course of action could strengthen the pro-Labor Party forces in the unions."

By breaking with the Democrats, as we urge, the Negro people can speed up the formation of a Labor Party. By sticking with the Democrats, as the Stalinists and Democrats advise, the Negro people can't change the present trend appreciably or at all let alone improve their conditions.

Let the Stalinists go into the Democratic Party if they wish. But don't let them mislead a single militant Negro or worker into following them! The job of militant Negroes and their white allies is to break with the capitalist parties, not to infiltrate those parties in the illusion that they can be reformed. Our job is to work for a Labor Party and to help guide the growing movement for Negro representation in office in such a way that it won't become swallowed up in the mire of capitalist politics.

SECTION II
WHAT IS INDEPENDENT POLITICAL ACTION?

This section features an article written by SWP National Secretary Farrell Dobbs on the campaign of Edward Atkinson, a Black candidate who ran in the nonpartisan primary for Los Angeles city council in 1959. Dobbs's article explains why socialists do not support Black Democratic Party candidates and explains the tactic of giving support to candidates that socialists have criticisms of.

One of the events referred to in Dobbs's article is the 1939 discussions between the exiled Russian revolutionist Leon Trotsky and Trinidadian-born writer C.L.R. James, who had been collaborating with the SWP leadership to advance its work fighting the oppression of Blacks. Excerpts from the discussion are contained in **Malcolm X, Black Liberation, and the Road to Workers Power** (Pathfinder Press, 2009). As an appendix to the Dobbs article we are reprinting a 1954 article by George Breitman entitled "Comments on the Trotsky-Johnson Discussion," which sought to refute the impression of some SWP members that Trotsky advocated support of Black Democrats.

Several of the references in this section may be unfamiliar to the reader. For information on the American Labor Party of New York and the Frankensteen campaign in Detroit, the reader can consult The Socialist Workers Party in World War II by James P. Cannon (Pathfinder Press, 1975) and Aspects of Socialist Election Policy (Socialist Workers Party, 1971).

Fundamental Aspects of the Atkinson Question
by Farrell Dobbs

Last March the Los Angeles branch recommended critical support to Edward Atkinson, a Negro candidate running for the City Council in the local primary elections. In asking the Political Committee's approval of this policy the comrades supplied the following information:

After a year's registration campaign among Negro voters in the Tenth Council-manic district a Citizens Committee nominated Atkinson against the incumbent, Councilman Navarro, a Mexican-American identified with the Republican Party machine. With the issue of Negro representation in office a key factor, the campaign aroused a strong response in the Negro community.

The elections are formally non-partisan. A Republican heads the Atkinson campaign committee, while the bulk of the committee is made up of Democrats. Atkinson, the candidate, is a Negro small businessman and a Democrat. He has not been prominent in politics and has not previously run for office.

Atkinson has described himself as a member of the Board of Directors of the Democratic Minority Conference, a local setup initiated by the Communist Party. The stated "Purposes and Objectives" of the DMC include: "To work with the organized Democratic Party. . . . To seek for ethnic and cultural minorities a voice in policy within the Democratic Party . . . to promote the general welfare of

Reprinted from *Aspects of Socialist Election Policy* (SWP, 1971)

the Democratic Party."

After weighing the above factors in the light of established party policy the PC on March 24 adopted the following motion: "As nearly as can be determined from available information, the Atkinson candidacy is too closely identified with the Democratic Party to warrant critical support."

In the April 7 primary elections Atkinson ran second in a field of five with 7,628 votes. Navarro led the field with 12,961 votes. A total of 29,570 votes were cast and the comrades figure about one third of these were Negro votes. There will be a run-off election between Atkinson and Navarro on May 26.

Comrades Milton Alvin and Lois Saunders asked the PC to reconsider its March 24 decision and approve critical support to Atkinson in the run-off election. In submitting their request they made extensive criticisms of the PC decision.

Charging the PC with a reversal of past policy, Comrade Saunders argues along these lines: "Up to now we have given critical support to minority candidates where the elections were non-partisan and where there was evidence that the candidate represented a serious community effort.... I know of no instance where the candidate gave any indication that he was breaking with capitalist class parties.... We supported the drive of the Negroes for representation, and this is all we supported. We criticized the programs as inadequate; we criticized the illusions of reliance on capitalist class parties; and we stressed the need for independent political action. *But we supported the candidates.*" (Her emphasis.)

Comrade Saunders thinks the PC has established a new criterion: ". . . namely that the campaign must be of such a nature as to indicate a break with capitalist parties . . . something borrowed from our work in the regroupment field. In socialist regroupment, a break with capitalist parties is a minimum requirement. It is incorrect, however, in my opinion, to confuse these two separate aspects of our activity and treat them as if they were one and the same thing where identical criteria apply."

To buttress her argument Comrade Saunders quotes extensively from the transcript of the 1939 Trotsky-Johnson discussion, seeking to clinch her point with the assertion: "Trotsky says that where a Negro Democrat is running we give critical support to the Negro, *not the Democrat.*" Emphasis is hers, not Trotsky's. Let us begin the examination of the question with this aspect of Comrade Saunders' argument.

To grasp the essential meaning of Trotsky's remarks about critical support to Negro candidates, it is necessary to recall that the Trotsky-Johnson discussion centered on the question of helping to form an independent Negro organization. As part of our effort to get the organization to adopt the most far-reaching program (transition measures), we would support the most militant wing. But among the leaders of this organization might be some with a Democratic background and the organization, against our urging, might decide to advance one of them as its candidate.

As members of the organization, what would we do in such a case? It would be possible under certain conditions, Trotsky thought, to offer the candidate critical support. What the conditions might be is not indicated in the transcript of the discussion (which remained uncorrected by the participants), but we may assume they would include control of the candidate by the Negro organization, plus his opposing Republican and Democratic candidates.

When understood in the full context of the Trotsky-Johnson discussion, the quotations cited by Comrade Saunders do not support her viewpoint. (See "Comments on the Trotsky-Johnson Discussion," by George Breitman.)

Looking further into the general question, one can only agree with Comrade Saunders' estimate that the running of Negro candidates is becoming a main avenue of struggle in the drive for full equality. Demands for a voice in Democratic Party policy, it may be added, also mark a new stage in the political development of the Negro movement. These changing conditions make our tactical problems more complex. But we must not forget that the problems remain two-sided. It is not alone a matter of adjusting our tactics to meet new conditions; we must be careful to maintain our basic principles.

The question of principles becomes increasingly obscured as Comrade Saunders further develops arguments in support of her tactical viewpoint. She contends: "We encourage Negroes in the South to register. . . . If we follow the PC line as regards Atkinson, we shall have to tell them after obtaining the right to vote, they should refuse to go to the polls and exercise that right, for virtually every candidate who will be running for office, whether Negro or white, will be either a Republican or a Democrat."

In reply let us consider some fundamentals. We support the right to vote no matter who the Negro voter may decide to back. At the same time we do not hesitate to say what political road we think the Negro movement should take and we do not go with them on the wrong road. This approach in no way contradicts the political necessities of the day. On the contrary, it is in accord with our basic task, our fundamental method, our whole reason for being as a revolutionary-socialist tendency.

We support the democratic demands of the Negro people even though they do not transcend the limits of the capitalist order. But we don't put democratic demands above class principles. At all times and under all circumstances we counterpose class struggle policies to class collaborationist illusions.

Merely to put a Negro candidate in office does not necessarily mean to advance the struggle for full equality. The democratic aspirations of the Negro people cannot be realized on the capitalist political road. The problem is rooted in a class question: what class shall the Negro people align themselves with in their freedom struggle?

Our first basic Negro resolution adopted in 1950 answered: "We must support this mass movement, develop it, and make it a politically conscious and definitely class movement. . . . The primary and ultimate necessity of the Negro movement is its unification with the revolutionary forces under the leadership of the proletariat." (*Fourth International*, May–June 1950, page 95.)

In line with this basic concept, we have given critical support to Negro candidacies only insofar as they represented independent political action in opposition to the capitalist parties. Formally non-partisan elections are not exempt from this criterion. They have particular significance only in the sense that they sometimes present a favorable vehicle for independent Negro political action.

Two examples from the past should suffice to illustrate that the question of critical support to Negro candidates has always centered on the issue of independence from the capitalist parties. In the spring of 1954 we gave critical support to the Turner candidacy in Newark, seeing it as a step toward independent Negro political action. A year later we made the opposite decision about the McCree and Robinson candidacies in Detroit. The latter two candidacies at first showed promise of being independent. Then the UAW-CIO brass moved in with the approval of the candidates and linked the campaign to the Democratic Party machinery for factional political purposes. With the Democratic-labor coalition thus acting to derail what had been a potential independent Negro campaign, we decided against critical support to McCree and Robinson.

Our criteria in deciding such tactical questions may be summarized as follows: We support the democratic demand of the Negro people for representation in government. We will give critical support to a Negro candidate—despite differences over program and despite the past connections of the candidate with the capitalist parties—provided the campaign represents a significant part of the Negro community and the candidate runs independent of and in opposition to the capitalist party machines.

We have always considered the question of crossing class lines in politics a matter of principle. Our policy has been to maintain unvarying class independence in political tactics. In accord with these conceptions the 1957 Negro resolution calls for: ". . . support to Negro candidates for public office so long as they run independently of the Democratic and Republican parties. . . . A labor-Negro alliance to launch an independent labor party based on the unions." (See *The Militant*, August 26, 1957, or the pamphlet "Class Struggle Road to Negro Equality.")

This aspect of party policy is recognized by Comrade Alvin in his criticism of the PC decision. He says: "Our attitude towards campaigns of this type (Atkinson) is guided by the idea of furthering independent politics for the labor movement and for the oppressed minorities. The principle that applies is the nature of the campaign itself, that is, is it genuinely independent of the capitalist parties in its dominant aspects."

However Comrade Alvin argues at length that

the PC has departed from our traditional position in determining whether a candidacy represents an independent political action. Much of his argument is based on the idea of proof through precedent. He cites the Alfange candidacy for governor of New York on the ALP ticket in 1942 and the CIO-backed Frankensteen candidacy for mayor of Detroit in 1945.

In both cases, Comrade Alvin accurately recalls, we gave critical support to the candidates on the basis of the independent nature of these labor campaigns as against the capitalist parties. His argument also puts major stress on the fact that we called Alfange a "Tammany hack," that Frankensteen had close ties with the Democratic Party and that the Democrats climbed onto the Frankensteen bandwagon toward the end of the campaign.

Comrade Alvin thinks Atkinson is not nearly so closely tied to the Democratic Party as was Frankensteen. On this premise he contends we were wrong in supporting Frankensteen in 1945 if we now refuse critical support to Atkinson on the ground he is too closely tied to the Democratic Party.

Once again let us consider some fundamentals. Tactical decisions do not derive one from another through the rule of precedent. Criteria deemed valid in one specific case do not automatically apply in another case.

Although tactics are generally designed to serve a specific current task or a given branch of the class struggle, in no field can tactical decisions be made without considering party perspectives as a whole. Our tactics must flow from and serve our central strategic aim, the building of a mass revolutionary party. Basic to this aim are our efforts to promote a mass turn from class collaborationist policies onto the class struggle road.

Our tactic of critical support to candidates running independently of the capitalist parties represents a transitional step toward the central strategic aim. For a number of historic reasons, we do not expect the initial mass break from capitalist politics to take place through the medium of the revolutionary socialist party. It is therefore necessary to adapt ourselves tactically to the actual forms through which independent political action develops. In doing so we seek to influence the movement in a revolutionary direction and to build up a revolutionary nucleus within it. The whole tactic is aimed toward building a mass revolutionary party. We must never forget that.

In every instance we must be clear about the basic purpose a particular tactic is intended to serve and we must weigh tactical decisions in terms of the given objective conditions and trends. Let us look again from this standpoint at our decisions to give critical support to Alfange and Frankensteen.

Both had a background of connections with the Democratic Party, a matter not to be taken lightly. What then were the considerations—in terms of the key facts and objective trends—that led us to extend critical support to their candidacies?

Alfange joined the ALP upon his nomination in 1942 as the party's candidate for governor. He ran in opposition to candidates of both the Democratic and Republican parties. As was their custom, the ALP backed several Democrats whose names appeared on both the Democratic Party and the ALP ballot lines. We supported none of these candidates on the ALP ballot. We gave critical support only to Alfange who ran as an independent ALP candidate in opposition to both capitalist parties.

Alfange got 400,000 votes, a significant demonstration of worker sentiment for independent class political action. This outcome became an important factor in the SWP's decision in 1943 to shift our advocacy of a labor party from a propaganda slogan to an agitational slogan. In doing so the party proceeded from a basic analysis of objective conditions and trends as appraised in the light of our fundamental aims. (See "Campaign for a Labor Party!" by James P. Cannon.)

In the same year the coal miners fought a series of heroic strike battles to break the war-time wage freeze. The year 1944 saw a general rise in labor unrest and a series of rank and file attempts to break through the official no-strike pledge. As the end of the war neared in 1945 a new, vast wave of working class struggle was building up.

In this objective setting the Frankensteen candidacy developed. It came at a time when unemployed demonstrations were sweeping the country and a half million workers were on strike. The General Motors strike was soon to trigger a general explosion that would see two million workers on the picket line at one time. Frankensteen's candidacy came on the heels of the 1945 victory of the British Labor Party and amid rising expressions of labor party sentiment in UAW-CIO locals, particularly in the Detroit area.

Frankensteen had ties with the Democratic Party, his candidacy had come on his own initiative and the Democrats climbed on the bandwagon at the last minute. That was one side of the picture. But he was also first vice-president of the UAW-CIO and he had been made the candidate of the Detroit CIO in a formally non-partisan election. The capitalist press, raising the alarm that the CIO was about to take over City Hall, stressed that the significance of his candidacy lay not in Frankensteen the individual but in Frankensteen the symbol. That was the other side of the picture.

Weighing both aspects of the question the Political Committee evaluated the Frankensteen candidacy as a borderline case where the decision might go either way. Because of the substantial weight of the trend toward independent class political action manifested in the campaign, a decision was made to give critical support. Present members of the PC who participated in the 1945 decision recall that it was expressly stated at the time that the decision should not be considered a precedent.

To evaluate party tactical decisions in the Alfange and Frankensteen cases the whole picture must be taken into consideration. One or another facet cannot be torn from context and used one-sidedly as an argument for critical support to the Atkinson candidacy today. The Atkinson question, like all tactical questions, must be appraised in the light of our fundamental aims as they apply to present objective conditions and trends.

Unlike the objective setting of the Frankensteen candidacy the present period is not characterized by great class battles giving rise to significant labor party sentiment. The labor-Democratic coalition line still dominates heavily in the unions and finds its echo in the Negro movement. Stalinist propaganda and devious CP maneuvers further disorient the mass politically.

These objective political factors must be considered alongside the democratic aspirations and the essential motion of the Negro movement. We must be clear not only on the issue of the independence of Negro candidates from capitalist politics. We must also be careful about rushing to characterize as independent a campaign where there is evidence it may in fact represent an attempt to play a greater role within a capitalist party.

In this connection we must examine carefully the role of the Democratic Minority Conference with which Atkinson has identified himself as a member of the Board of Directors. Nothing is explained when Comrade Alvin refers to this setup as a ". . . noisy but certainly not dominant section of the Democratic Party where the CPers have entrenched themselves."

The question is not one of dominance of this party of Big Business but of factional politics within it. Whether Atkinson is actually a leader of the DMC or is simply letting the CP use him and the Negro representation issue to push their pro-Democratic line, the result appears the same: political action within a capitalist party framework, not independent political action.

If we slur over questions of this kind in cases of Negro political action we can only introduce confusion into questions of independent labor political action. Policy in both spheres becomes intimately linked up through the need for a labor-Negro alliance to launch an independent labor party. Also directly involved are our basic aims and tasks in the 1960 presidential elections where the central issue will be independent political action in opposition to the capitalist political parties. We will be hurt in every field of activity if in any one of them we nibble at crossing class lines in politics.

We cannot subordinate basic considerations to the argument advanced by the comrades that failure to give Atkinson critical support will shut us out of the situation and give the Stalinists a clear field. We can't aspire to lead a movement if it is headed into Democratic Party politics. Our aim is to lead the fight for independent political action. For us two criteria are paramount: the nature of a given movement; and the direction in which it is going. We give critical support to a Negro candidate only where there is a break with capitalist politics and then only because the break implies a tendency toward independent class political action.

In fighting for this policy we have no reason to fear being in a minority or to look upon ourselves as being isolated from any chance to influence the mass movement. Our policy articulates the vital political needs of the Negro people. We have every reason to be aggressive in pushing our political line, to stand by our principled class position and to defend it vigorously against all opponent tendencies.

In general we must still act as the vanguard of the independent class political movement yet to come into being. But we can be confident mass discontent will grow and frustration will lead toward a break with capitalist politics. In the end we will be the big gainers from our consistent, principled vanguard role.

Our task now is to combine basic propaganda with action designed to help genuine independent political tendencies. In the process we will help to educate the best militants in class principles and to instill in them revolutionary consciousness. Wherever we can act to promote independent political actions the masses will be helped to realize they can build their own class political party apart from and in opposition to the capitalist parties.

In deciding to give critical support to a genuinely independent candidate we do not make programmatic agreement a condition. We support the break with capitalist politics as the first step toward independent class political action. But we do not hesitate to criticize errors and weaknesses in the program of the independent candidate and to advance our own program. Nor do we refrain from criticizing organizational weaknesses in the independent campaign in the sense of pointing the way toward an independent labor party built in alliance with the Negro movement.

Regarding the important role of the Negro movement in this key task, our 1957 Negro resolution said: "There are virtually no capitalists among the Negro people and only a thin layer of middle class elements. As a people they are overwhelmingly working class in composition. Taken nationally, a large section of the Negro workers are already unionized. These unionists are farthest advanced in connecting the fight for their civil rights with the struggle to defend their class interests and in raising political consciousness to a higher level. . . .

As yet the Negro movement is ahead of organized labor in gathering mass momentum. . . . When the workers act their struggles will lend fresh vigor to the Negro movement. This interrelation between the two movements will tend to lead them toward unity of purpose in the sphere of independent political action. . . .

Their fusion into a united political force would imply a head-on collision with the capitalist ruling class, breaking up the present two-party swindle and precipitating a class polarization in politics. In the process the civil rights forces could be expected to ally themselves with labor to launch an independent labor party based on the unions.

The passages quoted outline two transitional steps toward our central strategic aim, the building of a mass revolutionary party. These steps are: To help develop a working class political orientation within the Negro movement and promote a political alliance with labor as a class. To work for the creation of an independent labor party within which we would advocate adoption of a revolutionary socialist program.

This perspective clearly requires that we make independence from capitalist politics a criterion in giving critical support to Negro candidates. It also impels us to have the facts and a correct evaluation of the facts in determining whether a given candidacy is genuinely independent in character.

Fulfillment of these requirements, in the opinion of the Political Committee, was not established by Comrades Alvin and Saunders in their request for reconsideration of the decision on the Atkinson question. Consequently the PC on May 5 adopted the following motion: "To reaffirm decision that critical support of Atkinson candidacy is not warranted on basis of available facts."

Appendix: Comments on the Trotsky-Johnson Discussion
by George Breitman

For many years there has been confusion among comrades about the meaning of Trotsky's remarks on critical support of Negro candidates in the discussion held on April 11, 1939 (excerpts printed in *Malcolm X, Black Liberation, and the Road to Workers Power* (Pathfinder Press, 2009)). In the hope that no one will ever again interpret those remarks to mean that Trotsky was in favor of giving critical support to Negro candidates running on the Democratic ticket, here are the circumstances in which the remarks were made:

The discussion that day centered around a proposal that we should help form an independent mass Negro organization, a project that was generally favored, and around specific practical proposals for its formation, program, activity, etc. Under point 12 of the proposals, "The relationship of the Negroes to the Republican and Democratic parties," Trotsky said:

> How many Negroes are there in Congress? One. There are 440 members in the House of Representatives and 96 in the Senate. Then if the Negroes have almost 10% of the population, they are entitled to about 50 members, but they have only one. It is a clear picture of political inequality. We can often oppose a Negro candidate to a white candidate. This Negro organization can always say, 'We want a Negro who knows our problems.' It can have important consequences.

In the discussion that followed some participants expressed doubts and reservations about the permissibility of our supporting a Negro candidate run by the independent Negro organization whose formation had been projected. One voiced the fear, "Isn't it coming close to Popular Front, to vote for a Negro just because he is a Negro?" Another, answering this question, said, "This organization has a program. When the Democrats put up a Negro candidate, we say, 'Not at all. It must be a candidate with a program we can support.'" Then Trotsky said:

> It is a question of another organization for which we are not responsible, just as they are not responsible for us. If this organization puts up a certain candidate, and we find as a party that we must put up our own candidate in opposition, we have the full right to do so. If we are weak and cannot get the organization to choose a revolutionist, we might even withdraw our candidate with a concrete declaration that we abstain from fighting, not the Democrat, but the Negro. We consider that the Negro's candidacy as opposed to the white's candidacy, even if both are of the same party, is an important factor in the struggle of the Negroes for their equality; and in this case we can critically support them. I believe that it can be done in certain instances.

Let us repeat: the question being discussed was quite concrete—the running of a Negro candidate by an independent Negro organization (not just any Negro who happened to be a candidate). Trotsky was saying that we had the right to run our own candidate against the Negro candidate of such an independent Negro organization, but that we didn't have to employ this right under all circumstances. He also was saying that inside this independent Negro organization, when it got around to choosing the candidate it wanted to run, we would try to get it to nominate a revolutionist if possible, or a militant. If we failed in this inner nominating contest between ourselves and non-revolutionary tendencies inside the independent Negro organization, and if this organization chose instead a Negro who was a Democrat as its nominee, then we might decide to withdraw or not run a candidate of our own party against him in the general election, explaining that we took this action not because he was a Democrat in his politics but because he was a Negro candidate of an independent Negro organization. All this presupposes that

---

Reprinted from *SWP Discussion Bulletin*, Vol.20, No. 7, May 1959

this independent Negro organization's candidate is running against a white Democratic candidate, which is what Trotsky clearly meant when he said "both are of the same party."

The context plainly indicates that Trotsky was talking about critical support to the candidate of an independent Negro organization engaging in politics; to what we can properly call an independent Negro party running its own candidates against the candidates of the capitalist parties. This is exactly the policy that our party has been following for more than a decade. The only difference is that no single independent Negro organization running candidates has appeared in this country. (The largest Negro organization, the NAACP, does not formally run candidates in its own name.) What has happened generally is that a number of local Negro organizations get together and agree on or unite behind a candidate; instead of one independent Negro organization, there is usually a conference of several organizations, often on a temporary rather than a permanent basis. When that happens and their campaign represents a significant part of the Negro community and they run their own candidate against those of the capitalist party machines, it has been our practice to give him critical support, on the basis of the right of Negroes to representation in office, despite our differences with their program and despite the fact that the candidate may be a Democrat or a Republican in his politics. Our present policy, therefore, is in accord with the proposal made by Trotsky in 1939.

Trotsky was *not* talking about critical support to any Negro candidate; he was *not* talking about critical support to a Negro put up as a candidate by the capitalist parties; he was *not* talking about critical support to a Negro who had entered a capitalist primary election and won a capitalist party nomination with the support of the Negro community against the resistance of the capitalist party machine—he was talking about critical support to a Negro candidate of an independent Negro organization (or "party") running against capitalist party candidates.

I don't know if Trotsky knew the details about primary elections which are unknown in most of the world, or if he understood that entering primary elections meant entering capitalist parties. The point is that he did not consider this question at all in the 1939 discussion.

It may be argued by some comrades that we should give critical support to a Negro candidate of the Negro community who has won the nomination of a capitalist party in a primary election. But there is no valid reason whatever for claiming that such a position is supported by Trotsky's statements in the 1939 discussion, or in any other discussion or article known to us.

SECTION III. THE FREEDOM NOW PARTY

On June 1, 1963, at a street rally in Harlem, Black journalist William Worthy raised the idea of organizing an independent Black political party, a party whose banner would be "Freedom Now," a slogan of the growing civil rights movement. In August 1963, coinciding with the national march on Washington for civil rights, a call for the formation of a Freedom Now party was made, proposing an ambitious national election campaign in 1964, with the goal of obtaining 1 million votes.

While this call was received sympathetically by many, only in Michigan was the new party able to mount a serious electoral effort. Led by Rev. Albert B. Cleage, Jr., the Michigan Freedom Now Party was launched at an October 1963 rally in Detroit that projected a statewide campaign in the 1964 elections. Among the obstacles faced by the FNP were the attacks on it by many prominent Black and civil rights leaders who remained committed to the Democratic Party, including Dr. Martin Luther King, Jr. One Black leader who did express sympathy for the idea of an independent Black party was Malcolm X.

During the spring of 1964, the FNP petitioned for a place on the Michigan ballot and was subsequently certified. A slate of 39 candidates was fielded, headed by Cleage for governor and Ernest C. Smith for U.S. senator. Outside of Michigan, there were Freedom Now campaigns on a smaller scale in a few other places, including San Francisco, New Haven, and New York City.

The FNP had projected making a strong showing in the Michigan elections, but was able to obtain only several thousand votes. Cleage himself received 4,767 votes, or 0.2 percent of the total. The fact that the party had put such an emphasis on receiving a large vote, which did not materialize, led to demoralization among many of its activists. The FNP fell apart shortly after the elections.

This selection of articles begins with a section from the Socialist Workers Party's 1963 resolution entitled "Freedom Now," in which the SWP began to advocate the formation of an independent Black political party. The *Militant* article "Manifesto Issued in Capital for Freedom Now Party" describes the initial steps taken toward the formation of the FNP, and this article is followed by the two short documents that issued the call for the FNP in August 1963. The article in defense of the FNP was originally printed in the September 21, 1963, *Detroit Courier* and later reprinted in the *Militant*. LaMar Barron, acting chairman of the Michigan Committee for a Freedom Now Party, was also a member of the SWP. The next two selections, "FNP Files for Place on Michigan Ballot" and "Detroit SWP Candidate Withdraws in Favor of Freedom Now Nominee" were written during the course of the FNP's campaign and explain the SWP's attitude towards it. (The SWP was also successful in winning a place on the ballot for its slate of candidates in Michigan.) The next item reprinted, the Freedom Now Party Platform, was approved by the FNP state convention on September 20, 1964. The final two selections by George Breitman, written shortly after the elections, attempt to sum up some of the experiences and lessons of the FNP campaign.

The final article makes reference to the Mississippi Freedom Democratic Party. This organization made headlines through its attempt to be seated at the 1964 Democratic Party National Convention. Its goal, which was unsuccessful, was to replace the openly racist regular Mississippi Democratic organization and to become itself the official Mississippi affiliate of the Democratic Party.

Freedom Now
Excerpt from Resolution of Socialist Workers Party

The Negro struggle is above all a political struggle—that is, its solution requires political action. The coming labor-Negro alliance will operate in many areas and through many forms, but above all it will be a political alliance. And yet it is precisely in the field of politics that up to now practically all tendencies in the Negro movement are weakest and *least independent*, both in theory and practice.

Some tendencies ignore politics, but politics do not ignore them. The effect of political abstention is to leave the monopoly of political power in the hands of capitalist parties and demagogic politicians who use that power against the Negro people. Others recognize the importance of politics and participate in politics—but only in the two major parties that are opposed to Negro equality. Among politically active Negroes are some whose main interest is in electing Negroes to office. But these are repeatedly frustrated because the Negro Democrats or Republicans whom they help elect usually turn out to be captives and apologists for the corrupt capitalist political machines rather than consistent spokesmen for the Negro people.

Most current tendencies reflect, to one degree or another, the desire of the Negro masses to determine their own destiny—to have their own organizations, their own leaders, their own strategy, tactics and programs. But few of these tendencies have expressed a similarly independent spirit in the vital field of politics by breaking with the parties of their oppressors and organizing to challenge their political monopoly. Yet such a break and such a challenge are implicit in everything that has happened up to now. It is contradictory and self-defeating to talk about *Freedom Now* while accepting the right of the white supremacists and gradualists to jointly wield the political power of this country.

The idea of a Negro party, a civil rights party or an equal rights party, is not a new one. Representative Adam Clayton Powell has talked about it on and off during recent years. *Liberator*, the Liberation Committee for Africa magazine, wrote about the need for an "Afro-American political party" during the 1962 election campaign. More recently Elijah Muhammad, leader of the Muslims, has advocated that Negroes run and elect their own candidates to public office because "there will be no real freedom for the so-called Negro in America until he elects his own political leaders and his own candidates." William Worthy has spoken along similar lines.

The basis for such a party already exists. Millions of Negroes are concentrated in the big cities of the country, North and South. United in a party of their own, they are so situated geographically that they could sweep the elections in dozens of congressional districts. They could send a bigger bloc of Negroes to Washington than they did in Reconstruction days and elect a sizable body of state and city legislators who would for the first time be beholden to no one but the Negro community. Both nationally and locally they could hold the legislative balance of power and be in a position to compel bigger concessions from the dominant parties. More fundamentally, with a party of their own Negroes could take a lead in undermining and changing the whole power structure.

The immense implications of such an independent Negro course in politics illustrate graphically the truth of the revolutionary-socialist analysis that the independent Negro struggle tends to stimulate, spur and shake up the major forces in the country. The creation of a Negro party running its own candidates would rock the whole political structure to its foundations. It would throw the Democratic Party into a crisis. Without the majority of Negro votes which it now gets, it could never again hope to hold national power. The only place it could go would be down. Organized labor would be faced with an excruciating dilemma too. Its coalition with the Democrats is justified on the ground that the Democrats can "win." But when it becomes plain that they cannot win, the unions would be forced to reconsider their whole political policy. Advocates of a labor break with the old parties would get a bigger and better hearing from the ranks. Thus the creation of a Negro party would benefit not only the Negro but his present and potential allies.

The Socialist Workers Party contends that racism, like unemployment, exploitation and war, can be abolished in this country only by independent political action aimed at taking control of the government out of the hands of the capitalists and their parties. As a step in this direction, we have long advocated that the unions break from the Democratic Party and form an independent labor party that would seek to politically unite workers, farmers and Negroes and elect their representatives to office. In addition, and for the same reason, we have also endorsed and supported representatives of the Negro community whenever they have run for office independently of and in opposition to the old parties, even when they were not socialists.

Extending this policy in the light of current developments, we publicly express our readiness to support and collaborate with any Negro party or *Freedom Now Party* that runs candidates of its own in opposition to the capitalist parties and seeks to elect representatives whose primary allegiance will be to the Negro community. Our support of such a party in no way conflicts with our own independent socialist political campaigning or with our continued advocacy of a labor party. On the contrary, we believe that a Negro party, a socialist party, and a labor party would find much in common from the very beginning, would work together for common ends, and would tend in the course of common activity to establish close organizational ties or even merge into a single or federated party. Revolutionary socialists don't care whether capitalism and racism are abolished by a single party or by a combination of parties, just so long as they are abolished.

Manifesto Issued in Capital for Freedom Now Party
by Leslie Evans

WASHINGTON, D.C., Aug. 28—A call was issued here today for formation of a nation-wide, all-Negro Freedom Now Party which would run its first candidates in the 1964 elections.

Using the March on Washington as a launching pad for the new party, its organizers issued a stirring *Declaration of Washington* proclaiming the movement's aims and possibilities. (See full text below.) Simultaneously there was a distribution of leaflets calling for support in formation of the Freedom Now Party to the huge throngs of civil-rights demonstrators pouring into the capital.

Word that a call for a Negro party would be issued at the March on Washington leaked out a few days before and caused considerable stir. On Aug. 24 the *New York Times* carried a front-page story that such a call was going to be distributed to the marchers in Washington and added that on the same day "leaflets will also be distributed in Detroit, Chicago, Cleveland, San Francisco, Los Angeles, New York, Seattle and other cities with large Negro populations."

The *Times* also reported that a tentative national committee of the projected Freedom Now Party, under the acting chairmanship of civil-rights attorney Conrad Lynn, had opened an office at 81 East 125 St., in the heart of New York's Harlem.

The article reported Conrad Lynn as saying that he "had been in correspondence with many Negroes, active in civil-rights organizations who had indicated a strong receptivity to the idea of organizing a Negro Party."

In addition to the *Declaration of Washington*, a brochure has been released entitled "A Call For a Freedom Now Party." It asks,

> What sense does it make to go on supporting the party of Eugene (Bull) Connor? Bull Connor is still Kennedy's Democratic National Committeeman from Alabama.
>
> Why should Southern Negroes register to vote—at the risk of death—when the only

Reprinted from the *Militant*, September 2, 1963

'choice' on the ballot is a James O. Eastland or a George C. Wallace?

When have the Republicans or Democrats ever used long existing Federal laws to protect us from daily, coast-to-coast police brutality?

Our African brothers have shown us how to win freedom. Their principal technique: All black political action. This is self-reliance, not 'racism.'

"The times are with us," the brochure says. "A Freedom Now Party will for the first time unite us. We will be the permanent party of change and challenge. We will take the issues to the streets."

Lynn said the idea for an all-Negro party developed from a suggestion made by William Worthy, well-known Negro correspondent for the Baltimore *Afro-American,* at a June 1 street rally in Harlem.

Copies of the brochure are available from the National Committee for a Freedom Now Party, whose offices are at 81 East 125 St., Suite 207, New York, N.Y. 10035. Telephone 212 MO 2-0618. The brochures are listed at 15 cents for five copies; 50 cents for 20 copies. They also list Freedom Now Party buttons at 25 cents each.

A Call For a Freedom Now Party for 1964
with an All-Black Slate and a Platform for Liberation

WHY A FREEDOM NOW PARTY?

1. To at last *take* our freedom, with our own nationwide political party. Only once in all U.S. history has Congress passed, and the government enforced, *meaningful* equal rights laws. That was during Reconstruction when 25 Negro congressmen and 5 Negro senators sat in Washington. *Freedom Now!*

2. To create the basic economic changes needed to guarantee well-paid jobs for all. It's not enough to call for "equal opportunity" when jobs, decent housing, and schools are scarce even for whites. *Freedom Now!*

3. To end racism, exploitation, and colonialism—in Africa, Asia, Latin America—and in the United States, north *and* south. *Freedom Now!*

What sense does it make to go on supporting the party of Eugene "Bull" Connor? "Bull" Connor is *still* Kennedy's Democratic National Committeeman from Alabama.

Why should southern Negroes register to vote—at the risk of death—when the only "choice" on the ballot is a James O. Eastland or a George C. Wallace?

When have the Republicans or Democrats ever used long-existing federal laws to protect us from daily, coast-to-coast police brutality?

Our African brothers have shown us how to win freedom. Their principal technique: All-Black *political action. This is self-reliance, not "racism."*

The times are with us. A Freedom Now Party will for the first time unite us. We will be the permanent party of change and challenge. We will take the issues to the streets.

All blacks who wish to be free will be equal, and equally welcomed, as members: workers—employed and unemployed—clergymen, students, professional men and women, agricultural laborers, tenant farmers, trade union members.

To obtain worldwide moral support, copies of this brochure are being sent to all African, Asian, and Latin American delegates at the United Nations and to leaders of anti-colonial liberation movements everywhere.

This call for a Freedom Now Party is being distributed for the first time today, August 28, 1963, in Washington, D.C., and in black communities throughout the United States.

DECLARATION OF WASHINGTON

One hundred years after Lincoln's Emancipation Proclamation, we American Negroes are resolved

---

Reprinted from the *Militant,* September 2, 1963

to end all political dependence upon the political parties upholding segregation and to take our destiny in our own hands.

Our way to freedom and equality is through all-black political action. Our way to unity is through the creation of a Freedom Now Party.

What can a national all-Negro political party expect to achieve?

It will concentrate the voting power of black Americans in a single organization that can deliver knock-out punches to the enemies of equality.

It can put genuine representatives, responsible to the Negro people, in office all the way from local communities to Washington.

Unchained to vested interests, the Freedom Now Party can promote basic economic changes that will give everyone adequate employment, housing and education. It can carry forward the struggle for jobs and justice, not only at election times but all the year round.

It can win at least a million votes in 1964.

It will certify that the Negro has come of age. If our African brothers can win independence, freedom and self-government, why cannot we American Negroes assert similar capacities for political action and achievement? Moreover, the new party will be the natural voice of fraternity with the oppressed of Africa, Asia and Latin America who are also striving to end racism, exploitation and colonialism.

One hundred years of waiting for Democratic and Republican politicians to correct our grievances is too long. We have to *take* our freedom; no one will hand it to us.

Appeal to youth

That is why, in the nation's capital, on this occasion of the greatest civil-rights demonstration in American history, we call upon all who believe in true emancipation to join us in forming and building the Freedom Now Party. We appeal especially to those courageous young Negroes in the South and in the city ghettos who are teaching their elders the meaning of today's fight for freedom.

This Party has been initiated by Negroes. All of its candidates will be black. But we are not anti-white. Our banner is not "racism" but self-reliance. We are the political expression of the mighty black crusade for freedom that nobody can now halt or suppress.

Today the Negro is at the bottom of the power structure. As he rises, he cannot help but lift the status of every other fellow-American who suffers from existing evils. In the name of 20 million black Americans, we aspire to transform the United States into a happier, freer, more democratic country that the rest of the world will admire and not despise or fear.

The first step will be the founding of our Party. We call on all Negroes or their representatives to join in a historic founding congress and to build the Party in every possible way.

The Freedom Now Party is the next indispensable step. United in our own Party, militant in our action, uncompromising in our principles—

We Shall Overcome.

A million votes for freedom now!

In Defense of Move for Freedom Now Party
by LaMar Barron

The ink was hardly dry on the call for the formation of an all-black Freedom Now Party before various critics, white and Negro, began popping off.

Robert C. Ruark, the novelist, is well-known for his hate, contempt and slanderous distortions of the African freedom struggles. But that doesn't stop him from writing a condescending column (*Detroit Free Press*, Sept. 6) telling us what we can and cannot do, and what we should and should not do, in our freedom struggle here.

When Negroes get together and try to improve

Reprinted from the *Militant*, September 30, 1963

our lot through our own resources, he condemns our self-reliance as "reverse discrimination" and warns us, ominously, that this is "dangerous."

Dangerous to whom? To what?

An all-black political party, he pontificates, is a "return to discrimination." But how can there be a "return" to something that hasn't left or been ended? Let discrimination be truly abolished (and not just talked about) and the Ruarks won't have to worry about us organizing against the discriminators.

Justified feeling

Meanwhile, as long as discrimination continues, we intend to use the justified racial feeling of Negroes to promote the elimination of discrimination. What's wrong with that?

The *New York Times* is even more upset than the Ruarks. Its editorial against the Freedom Now Party (Aug. 26) is entitled "Racism in Politics." It is long on invective and short on argument. It seems to be trying to make two points:

One is that "the United States is not Africa" and that all-black political action worked in Africa because blacks are a majority there and can't work in the U.S. because we are a minority here.

Profoundly brilliant! We don't know how we could get along without these clever editorial writers.

But we never said or pretended we are a majority in this country. What we say is that a minority can exert political power too if it is united and bold and stops letting its own power be used by its proven enemies.

If we organize our own party, it will shake the whole political structure of this country from top to bottom.

There would no longer be a *majority* political party. New alignments and alliances would have to take place. Negro political power would then count for something, because with our own party we would be able to use it for our own benefit.

Bigwigs know

The Democratic bigwigs know this. That's why they are upset even by *talk* about a Freedom Now Party.

The other *Times'* argument is that the labor movement doesn't have a labor party, so why should the Negro movement have a Freedom Now Party?

All I can say to that is that labor *should* have its own party. It is the only labor movement in the world that doesn't have a party of its own, and that is why it is so politically weak and on the defensive.

I predict that labor will form its own party after we form ours, because after we leave the Democratic Party it will become a permanent minority party, and labor will see no further point in hanging onto the Democratic coattails.

I also predict that a Freedom Now Party and a labor party will cooperate because they will have common enemies and many common goals.

A Negro weekly newspaper has chimed in too. "All-Negro Party A Step Backwards" is the title of its editorial.

The Negro weekly sees no hope for the Negro unless he "joins with the white liberal." It thinks anything else is "illogical . . . impractical . . . political suicide."

I am afraid that the brothers at the Negro weekly still don't know what the present massive black revolt is all about. If our revolt means anything, it is our rejection and repudiation of the white liberals, whom we have permitted for too long to dictate what we ask for, when, where and how.

If our fate depends on our remaining "joined" to the white liberals and letting them have veto power over our struggle, we might as well give up now and resign ourselves to being buried in our grave as a slave.

Proposal

All the Negro weekly has to propose politically is that Negroes increase their "voting strength in the two major parties." At the same time they lament the fact that "in the North many Negroes feel they have nothing for which to vote."

The only reason many Negroes feel that way is because it's so. Neither of the major parties has anything to offer Freedom Now fighters; that's why so many of us go fishing on election day. But a Freedom Now Party will generate political enthusiasm and activity on a mass scale in the Negro ghetto, North and South. Because it will stand for something the people want.

Finally, we take note of the contribution to the

discussion by Roy Wilkins, NAACP secretary. Speaking over radio in New York (Sept. 8), Wilkins said:

> I would hate to see a racial, purely racial political action in this country. I think it would be unfortunate if we had a white party and it would be equally unfortunate to have a black party.

Present setup
Well, we have white-controlled parties now, and that certainly has worked out in an unfortunate way. But why, with white-controlled parties blocking our way to freedom, would it be "equally unfortunate" to have a black-controlled party striving for our freedom?

Brother Wilkins did not say, at least in the article I read. But he said something even more revealing—that a "Negro political party might have some value in the South on a local basis."

Why? Because "they've been the victims of racism in the South and so it makes sense down there." But if it makes sense for Southern victims of racialism, why doesn't it also make sense for Northern victims? Or is Brother Wilkins contending that we in the North are not victims of racialism?

Whatever way you look at it, his argument doesn't make much sense. But that often happens when "Negro leaders" try to parrot white arguments against independent action and self-reliance by the Negro.

They say politics makes strange bedfellows. This surely is confirmed by the mental antics of the unholy crew lining up against the Freedom Now Party.

FNP Files for Place on Michigan Ballot
by George Breitman

DETROIT, May 2—The Freedom Now Party yesterday filed petitions with 19,892 signatures for a place on the Michigan ballot next November. Additional signatures were to be submitted in Lansing tomorrow, the last day for filing.

The names of 14,896 registered voters are needed to qualify a new political party for ballot status in this state. It may be weeks before the secretary of state's office announces the number of signatures which it declares to be valid.

Michigan is the first state in the country where the all-black Freedom Now Party has filed on a state-wide basis. The Michigan section of the FNP was organized last October.

Today's *Detroit Free Press* reported that the filing had produced "some consternation among Democratic politicians." The *Detroit News* quoted Secretary of State James M. Hare, a leading Democrat, as saying that "the Freedom Now Party might get up to 100,000 votes with its program of 'independent black political action.'"

Rev. Albert B. Cleage, state chairman of the FNP, added to the consternation by saying that his party expects to submit a full slate of Negro candidates in the Nov. 3 election.

"We will have a candidate for governor and for all other elective state offices," he said. "We also expect to have candidates for the state legislature, Wayne County offices and maybe three or four seats in Congress."

In recent elections the Democrats have been getting as high as 80 to 85 per cent of the vote in Negro districts. If enough Negro voters desert the Democrats for the Freedom Now Party, the Democrats will be in a bad way, and political life will get shaken up quite a bit in this state.

The Democrats may be consternated, but they are not too surprised. They have been biting their nails since the FNP announced its petition campaign last October.

More than that. They have also been conducting a real hate campaign against those Negroes who

Reprinted from the *Militant*, May 11, 1964

have the nerve to think that their votes don't belong, forever and ever, to the Democratic machine, or to the Republican machine, and who propose to mobilize the Negro vote around a party that will be led by Negroes, controlled by Negroes and responsible to nobody but the Negro community.

Although the Freedom Now Party is only a few months old, it has already been given the full treatment of slander and misrepresentation that is reserved for truly independent parties. It has been accused—falsely—of advocating violence, being subversive, acting like wild lunatics and simple-minded utopians, preaching black supremacy, wanting to go back to Africa, helping the Republicans, disuniting the Negro community; everything in the book, with the exception, possibly, of wife-beating.

The whites who control the Democratic Party don't have to spread these slanders themselves—they have plenty of Negroes who will do it for them. One of the worst offenders is a man with a hitherto fine record, Rev. Charles A. Hill, pastor of the Hartford Baptist Church.

Had won respect

Hill has had, and has earned, respect for his courage in standing up to the House Un-American Activities Committee, in defending the rights of all, including the Communist Party, in speaking out against racism, war and regimentation. In the late 1940s he had the endorsement of the Socialist Workers Party when he ran for the city council.

But what he is doing now is really pathetic. He has helped to form a group, Volunteers for Lyndon B. Johnson, and is doing everything he can to discredit the Freedom Now Party. In one case he prevailed on another preacher to cancel the use of his church for an FNP meeting against police brutality. Last month he took the lead in getting the influential Baptist Ministers Conference to condemn the Freedom Now Party and the Group on Advanced Leadership (GOAL) for spreading "violence, bitterness and hatred."

Hill was quoted as saying, "I say to these crazy people among us that we don't want them. If they want all-black, they should pack up and go to Africa. We should close our churches to them."

He is a living example, and a sad one, of people who until recently were in the forefront of the Negro struggle, but have now been swept off their feet and bypassed by its stormy new manifestations. They can't understand what has happened to the thinking of the younger forces in the struggle, they can't adust themselves to the new pace and the new demands, they become shrill and incoherent, and some of them end up sounding something like the Uncle Toms they themselves have fought for so long.

If the Freedom Now Party is certified for the Michigan ballot, it will have the fifth row. The top two are occupied by the capitalist parties, the Socialist Workers Party has the third row, and the Socialist Labor Party the fourth.

Lovell's view

In a statement today, Frank Lovell, state chairman and candidate for governor of the Socialist Workers Party, said:

> Instead of consternation, we feel gratification about the Freedom Now Party filing its petitions, and we hope that public opinion will prevent any Democratic monkey-business such as challenging their validity.
>
> The Socialist Workers Party is in this campaign to fight and expose the Democrats and Republicans as the agents of big business, racism and reaction. We are not campaigning against the Freedom Now Party, which in our view has valuable contributions to make to the electoral struggle for a world free of oppression and exploitation. We welcome its entry into the election campaign, and hope it will get a fair hearing from whites as well as Negroes.
>
> Our only regret is that the labor movement hasn't broken from the old parties and asserted its political independence too. Let's hope that the independent example set by the Freedom Now Party will be contagious, catch on among white workers, and give birth to a labor party.

Detroit SWP Candidate Withdraws in Favor of Freedom Now Nominee

DETROIT—The Wayne County Convention of the Socialist Workers Party on Sept. 12 decided to endorse the full county ticket nominated by the Freedom Now Party.

Delegates to the convention voted unanimously in favor of a motion that the SWP "not run candidates for State Senate, State Legislature or Wayne County offices," and that the party "support and actively campaign for the Freedom Now Party candidates in these races."

Richard T. David, who had previously announced his candidacy in the 23rd State Legislative District and had campaigned extensively, declared his withdrawal in favor of Hugh Cleage, Freedom Now Party candidate in that district.

Important step

Said David:

> The formation of the Freedom Now Party, in my opinion and in the opinion of the Socialist Workers Party, is an important step forward for the black people of this state . . .
>
> As long as working people and black people remain tied to either of the old parties, there can be no real progress toward racial equality, jobs for all, economic security, or peace.
>
> The unions ought to break with the old parties and create an independent labor party, instead of being a tail to the Democratic donkey. The Negro people ought to turn their back on the old parties too, create their own party, and run their own representatives for office who will be independent of the old party machines and responsible only to the Negro community.
>
> The Freedom Now Party has taken the first step in this direction . . . I welcome this step and want to encourage it. I am withdrawing from the 23rd District race in order to unite the anti-Democratic and anti-Republican vote behind the Freedom Now Party candidate. It so happens there is no Republican in this race. When I withdraw there will be only the Freedom Now Party candidate, Hugh Cleage, and the Democratic Party candidate, Maxine Young. Mrs. Young represents a party that has betrayed the Negro people over and over again. I urge the voters to vote for and elect her Freedom Now Party opponent on Nov. 3.

The Michigan SWP is holding its convention Sept. 19 to nominate its candidates for state-wide offices and to file its national ticket—Clifton DeBerry for President and Edward Shaw for Vice President.

Reprinted from the *Militant*, September 21, 1964

The FNP Platform

PREAMBLE

We, the black people of the State of Michigan, and of these United States, in this historic period of worldwide revolutionary change, recognizing our desire to achieve our own destiny through our own efforts; recognizing our desire for independent black political action after 188 years of political subservience; recognizing that our struggle for freedom and equality can issue, meaningfully, only from our own leadership and candidates, do establish the only independent political movement dedicated to the unity and liberation of all black people—the *Freedom Now Party!*

The *Freedom Now Party*, in its dedication, per-

Reprinted from the *Militant*, October 5, 1964

ceives the common interests of black people everywhere and, as a united body of Afro-Americans, aligns itself with all liberation movements throughout the world!

The *Freedom Now Party*, in its recognition of its mandate repudiates and breaks with the established party system which serves only to sustain the enslavement of Afro-Americans!

The *Freedom Now Party*, in its awareness of history, is not a reform movement. The condition of the Negro in America cannot be altered by reform. It must be fundamentally changed!

The *Freedom Now Party*, in its understanding of the needs of black people, is an educational as well as a political movement. It is a medium for the awakening of Afro-Americans to political and historic consciousness; and it is a vehicle for them to do something about it!

As our Declaration of Washington, on Aug. 28, 1963, on the founding of the *Freedom Now Party* states, "We are the political expression of the mighty black crusade for freedom that nobody can halt or suppress." All black people everywhere are welcome to join us in this momentous and historical undertaking for

FREEDOM NOW

Title I—Police Brutality

The *Freedom Now Party* intends to use all of the political power it will generate to eradicate this vicious practice that has so long been used to deny the Negro his basic equality.

Title II—Civil Rights Commission

The *Freedom Now Party* intends to demand that this constitutional commission with its vast powers carry out its constitutional powers and make real its constitutional directive. We note that the principal areas of concern are equal opportunities in employment, education, housing and public accommodations.

Title III—Inadequate representation in government by the Negro

The *Freedom Now Party* deplores the lack of representation in government. The *Freedom Now Party* feels that we must solve this problem ourselves with the instrumentality of independent black political action. We understand that a Democrat represents Democrats, a Republican represents Republicans, but that a *Freedom Now Party* candidate represents Negroes.

Title IV—Economic Plight

The *Freedom Now Party* understands that in this society the fundamental area of our exploitation is economic. We therefore shall strive in every way to utilize the total power of the Negro community and to bring it to bear upon the discrimination that places us at the bottom of the economic ladder. Our concern is for our own black people and we consider the solution of this problem as more important than the economic theories of this society or the peace and tranquility of this society.

Title V—Schools

The *Freedom Now Party* demands schools of the highest quality for black children. It is our belief that this is a multi-racial society and within that context the schools must involve themselves with the realities of that situation. For black children this means that Negro history must be taught and the future must be depicted as a process in which the black man and the white man share the stage as equals.

Title VI—Political

The *Freedom Now Party* is the expression of independent black political action and the political arm of the Negro's struggle for *freedom now*.

What the Freedom Now Party Has Accomplished
by George Breitman

DETROIT, Nov. 13—Under unfavorable conditions, the Freedom Now Party of Michigan accomplished at least two things on election day: It managed to survive the Democratic landslide, which was more like a hurricane in Negro areas. And it introduced into Michigan politics the new idea that the Negro community should break with both major parties and organize independently of them in a party controlled by and responsible to itself.

On election night, the combined newspaper-radio-TV service collecting returns from throughout the state repeatedly reported over the air that Rev. Albert B. Cleage, FNP candidate for governor, had received over 19,000 votes, with less than two-thirds of the total tallied. Since then, however, the same agency refuses to confirm that figure, or even explain it, saying that the Cleage total was only 4,620. Official results may not be available until the end of the month, and FNP attorneys were considering court action to compel a recount if it could be done inexpensively.

There are an estimated 260,000 Negroes registered to vote in Michigan, according to Roy Wilkins of the NAACP. Allowing for the fact that not all of those registered actually voted, and allowing also for the fact that some whites voted for him, Cleage's vote represented approximately nine per cent of the Michigan Negroes who voted on election day, if it was in the 19,000 range; and approximately two per cent if it was the lowest figure cited. Candidates for the state legislature from Wayne County districts varied from two per cent to one-half per cent.

While not spectacular, even a two per cent figure for Cleage is a creditable achievement when all the circumstances are considered.

The political circumstances were about as bad as they could be for a new party. Among Negroes the fear and hate of Goldwaterism was greater than in any other section of the population. Although they have always voted overwhelmingly for the Democrats since the depression of the 1930s, this time it was practically unanimous for Johnson.

Michigan is one of the states where by pulling a single lever you can vote a straight-party ticket, and that is the way most black and white workers vote here. Democratic campaign workers stationed at every precinct warned voters not to "take any chance of messing up your ballot" by splitting their vote. The FNP urged Negroes to pull down the "straight-FNP" lever (for 17 statewide candidates and up to eight others in Wayne County) and then go to another line to vote their choice for president, for which the FNP had no candidate. Instead, most Negroes, wanting above all to vote for Johnson, pulled the straight-party lever for the Democrats.

But even if the Democratic sweep and the straight-ticket tradition here were not so strong, the obstacles facing the FNP were enormous.

This was the first time in the entire history of the country that an independent Negro party had appeared on state-wide ballot. The idea was so new, so bold, so unconventional, that it shocked most people, including most Negroes.

The FNP's task, of course, was not made easier by the torrent of lies poured on it by virtually every political tendency in the state. The capitalist press, the strong labor movement and every "respectable" Negro leader in Michigan lied, attacked, ridiculed and lied again about the FNP.

The FNP was charged with being racist, with being a "Muslim" group, with opposing integration, with favoring a separate Negro nation, with advocating violence. The liberal Democrats added the lie that it was secretly working on behalf of the Republicans, and the Uncle Toms chimed in with the lie that it was trying to "divide" the Negro community.

In the last week of the campaign the Democrats and the UAW leadership brought Martin Luther King, Adam Clayton Powell, Bayard Rustin, Norman Hill and Aaron Henry into Detroit to do last-minute hatchet-jobs on the FNP. The FNP leaders fought back vigorously and militantly, but these people have considerable prestige in the Negro

Reprinted from the *Militant*, November 23, 1964

community and there is no doubt that they did damage to the FNP vote.

The first serious effort to lead the Negro people out of the clutches of the capitalist two-party system deserved the sympathy and aid of every radical organization, but with the exception of the Socialist Workers Party and the Young Socialist Alliance, no support was given by any radical group in Michigan.

On the contrary, they endorsed the lies and spread them, as though they subscribed to the notion that the Negro vote "belongs" to the Democrats in the same way that a slave belongs to a slaveholder. The Communist Party put heavy pressure on Negroes under its influence not to have anything to do with the FNP under any circumstance.

In addition to the misrepresentation and hostility of these forces, the FNP has had to contend with a fact that cannot be stressed too much: The attempt to create an independent party represents a break with tradition and precedent so sharp that in the beginning the very idea was "unthinkable" except for the most advanced forces.

Incomplete picture

As a result of both these factors, most Negroes in Michigan still have not gotten a clear and complete idea of the FNP and its aims. Most of them now have heard something about the FNP, which means they have had to think about it to some degree, however briefly and inadequately. That is not the same thing as 1) fully understanding what the FNP stands for, or 2) agreeing with it. But it is a first step in that direction. To really appreciate the difficulties of that first step, some knowledge of the FNP's history would be helpful.

The FNP was started in August, 1963, through a "call" by a number of black intellectuals in New York. It was to be a national party, and small groups were soon formed in several areas (during October in Michigan). But for various reasons these groups did not pass beyond the area of discussion. Only in Michigan did the local group undertake the hard work of getting on the state ballot in 1964. Some of the local groups still exist, but most of the national initiators dropped away or became inactive.

The Michigan group was formed in the belief that it would get the advice and help of a national party and a national leadership. Instead, it was thrown on its own resources. While this worked out positively in some ways, stimulating local initiative and experiment, it was a handicap in other ways.

Much has been written nationally about "what the FNP stands for," but most of it is nonsense, even when the writers are not completely biased, because the FNP has not yet held any convention, national or regional, to pool ideas and arrive at common positions. It therefore has neither a national program, a national leadership nor a national organizational structure. (Some draft platforms were written in New York in the early part of the year, but they were never accepted by any conference and represented only individual opinions rather than the position of the party.)

So the Michigan FNP has had to go it alone, without political collaboration or aid from a national movement. This made a hard job harder. All the important political issues are national and international; hardly any can be solved in a single state. The Michigan FNP was not prepared to write a national program, but without one its activities suffered, both externally and internally. For the absence of a national program and a national organization raised vital questions about the nature and direction of the Michigan FNP that have never been completely settled.

In Michigan the FNP is now around a year old. Its first six months were devoted almost entirely to petition-gathering. The other sides of normal political activity—education, recruiting of new members, spreading of propaganda and, above all, working out a program to unite the members and inspire them for the long haul—were subordinated to getting on the ballot. If it had been done differently, perhaps the FNP would not have got on the ballot this year; but doing it this way helped to create or sharpen problems that came to the fore later.

Because the FNP won ballot rights by collecting 22,000 signatures, many people, outside Michigan especially, got the impression that it is larger numerically than it is actually is. The truth appears to be that the membership runs in the hundreds, not the thousands, and the number of dependable activists is smaller than that.

Besides being a relatively small organization taking on a gigantic job, the FNP suffered from inexperience, as Rev. Cleage was the first to point out publicly. Very few of its leaders or members had ever held posts of responsibility or authority in any political party, where they could acquire or develop political talents and organizational know-how. As a result, some mistakes were unavoidable.

Members of other minority political groups tend, I think, to underestimate this factor. They have seen how new people come into their organizations absolutely green, without any previous political or organizational background, and often are able in a few months to make big contributions and play leading roles.

What they overlook is the difference between coming into an established organization *with a tradition,* generally accepted ways of doing things, and a leadership of some continuity that can transmit the lessons of past experiences and mistakes to new members—and coming into an entirely new organization without a tradition, without agreed-on methods of operating, without accumulated experience, without an experienced leadership, with almost all questions of policy and organization still open and to be decided. It makes quite a difference.

In May, after the party was certified for the ballot, it was gripped by an internal factional struggle produced by inexperience, impatience, personality clashes and uncertainty over what kind of structure and program the party should have.

Disputes and struggles are part of the process of growth, inevitable in any democratic organization. They also can be educational, even beneficial, if programmatic differences underlying them can be formulated clearly and then debated and resolved on their merits.

But if programmatic differences were the underlying cause of this particular struggle, they remained obscure and were never clearly expressed by anyone. Instead the dispute took the form of opposition versus support to the FNP leadership centered around Rev. Cleage. This was partly because of the way the party had been organized.

No convention was held at the beginning to elect a leadership. A few people came together—few because not many were willing to stick their necks out at that point—and, in order to get a petition campaign going without delay, designated themselves as a state committee, with Cleage as chairman. Their justification for this procedure was that if they waited until an organization was built, until discussion was held, until officers were elected, the FNP would not get on the ballot this year.

Nobody questioned this arrangement until the internal dispute began, when the authority of the state committee (to set the rules for organizing the first state convention) was challenged. Eventually the members democratically voted by a decisive majority to uphold the state committee's authority.

But some of the bitterness and suspicion continued, almost paralyzing the party during four precious months when it should have been clarifying and completing its program, selecting its candidates and launching its election campaign. Valuable time and opportunity were lost until late September when the first FNP state convention was held, and candidates were chosen, a state platform adopted, and a state committee elected. Only then, 45 short days before the election, did the members close ranks and begin to put together their campaign apparatus.

No other party in the campaign, major or minor, operated under such a handicap. What might have been done in five or six months could not be done in one and a half. The party rallied to the occasion and campaigned valiantly, but its effectiveness was limited.

It was limited mainly by the over-all political situation—and by lack of money, fewness of campaign workers and other factors over which the party had little control. It was limited also by uncertainty, confusion and illusions among some of the party members, including some candidates.

An illustration was the state platform adopted by the state convention (reprinted in the Oct. 5 *Militant*). It has a number of good points, but on the whole it is characterized by vagueness; it is very general. Read by someone unfamiliar with the FNP, it raises more questions than it answers. Explanation was the crying need, and it does not explain very much.

I have heard it said that the platform was deliberately vague—in order to make it broader in appeal. But it didn't work out that way. Uncertainty about important unresolved questions was continued, not cleared up. This became reflected in one-sided and inconsistent statements by some of the candidates during the campaign.

Some made it seem that forcing concessions from the major parties (such as their nomination of a Negro for lieutenant-governor next time) was the chief *aim* of the FNP, while others more correctly spoke of such concessions as a *result*, as a by-product, of a large FNP vote. Some emphasized primarily the need to elect black candidates, without enough concrete attack on the black candidates of the major parties. A few wanted to have the FNP support Johnson, in order to get more votes.

Blurred image

Even the racial character of the party became blurred in the campaign. The practice so far has been to keep the membership all-black, but the state convention failed to deal with this question (as with others). At least two candidates said during the campaign that the FNP is not all-black, that anyone is welcome to join. This tended to create the impression that spokesmen of the party were insincere or did not know what they were talking about.

More understandable, but also wrong, was the illusion held by some of the leaders about the number of votes they would get at the polls. They thought that Negroes, once in the privacy of the booth, would be unable to vote against a party bearing the name of "Freedom Now." Several candidates seriously expected to get elected, and spent most of their money on posters bearing names and a slogan or two, and not enough on literature refuting the lies about the party. (The printed campaign propaganda was on the weak side, not matching the educational quality of speeches by Cleage, Milton Henry and some others.)

The same illusion about the vote may account for insufficient attention to routine party-building, recruiting and educational activity. Some thought that the way to build the party was to roll up a big vote and elect some candidates, after which new members would flock in. It is plain now that building a mass party is not that easy; it can't be done through a few weeks of electioneering, but needs sustained activity on many fronts throughout the year.

Such weaknesses, which can be overcome with further experience, may explain why the FNP vote was not bigger. But they must be seen in correct perspective, for they do not in any way alter the undeniable achievement of the FNP campaign: Against the hurricane the FNP stood firm and fearlessly expounded the basic principle that had brought it into existence—independent black political action.

Unshaken by the prevailing winds of opportunism and expediency, the FNP raised and militantly defended the banner of Negro political independence. The banner did not attract as many recruits as FNP members hoped, but it is still flying. And it will be there, as a rallying center, when the masses begin to taste the bitter fruits of the Democratic victory and realize they have been rooked again.

Most Negroes were not convinced this time. But a new idea has been planted in their minds, and they will have occasion to think about it again. Meanwhile, at least two per cent of the Negro voters already have given it their support at the ballot box—an idea none of them would have dreamed of two years ago. If these two per cent can be recruited, educated and activated, the FNP's second campaign will be many times bigger and better than its first.

It will be better in any case. From all indications, the members have learned many lessons from this campaign; the leadership passed a hard test and its authority has risen; and the party as a whole, far from being disheartened, is confidently facing the future and already preparing its next steps.

One final point: To evaluate the contribution made by the FNP and to measure the stature of its leadership, one need only compare them with the nationally better-known Negro leaders and the infinitely more powerful union leaders. One and all, the latter capitulated disgracefully to the Democrats and were swept away in the Democratic flood. The FNP leaders stand head and shoulders above them all; they represent the politically most advanced tendency in the whole Negro movement; they set an example that all of the mass movement will have to follow sooner or later. For this they have earned the thanks and deserve the support of everyone who hates oppression and exploitation.

Further Discussion on Freedom Now Party
by George Breitman

I

DETROIT—Some people have questioned my opinion that the Freedom Now Party of Michigan represented "the politically most advanced tendency" in the whole Negro movement at the time of the Nov. 3 election. "What about the Mississippi Freedom Democratic Party?" I have been asked. "Isn't that another political tendency with great promise? Aren't you underestimating its significance, and thereby the significance of the Southern struggle as a whole?"

My answer should begin by stating that I do not question the dedication of the Mississippi FDP leaders to the cause of Negro freedom, or their courage. The question is whether their policy in relation to the Democratic Party is correct or "advanced."

The problems in the South are different in many respects from those in the North. In Mississippi, Negroes are denied the right to register and to vote. In Michigan, as in the rest of the North, that is no problem. In Mississippi, the Democrats don't want Negroes in their party and are trying to keep them out. In Michigan, the Democrats are anxious to keep Negroes in their party. The *tactical* situation is therefore quite different.

Negroes now have formed political organizations *outside* the Democratic Party in both Mississippi and Michigan. In Mississippi, the aim of the new organization (FDP) is to force its way into the Democratic Party—either as a part of the state Democratic Party or as the unit recognized by the national Democratic Party as its Mississippi section. In Michigan, the aim of the new organization (FNP) is to win Negros away from the Democratic Party (and away from the Republican Party) and create, a new, independent, Negro-controlled center speaking and acting for Negroes in politics.

In both cases, the *form* of the organization is independent. But in Mississippi, the *essence* is not independent—the FDP seeks to become part of the national Democratic Party in one way or another, because it thinks the Democratic Party can be reformed. In Michigan, both the form and the essence were independent in the recent election campaign of the FNP, which proceeded from the view that the Democratic Party cannot and will not serve as a political agency for Negro liberation.

This is the point from which thinking must start if you want to decide which policy is most advanced. If you think that Negro equality can be won through the Democratic Party, that the Democratic Party can be reformed enough to become a dependable instrument of the Negro freedom movement, then of course you will support and work inside the Democratic Party; and you will reject the FNP's policy as wrong and harmful, in Michigan as well as Mississippi.

But if you think that the Democratic Party, like the Republican Party, is and always will be an obstacle to Negro equality, then you will agree that it is futile to work inside it and that the indicated course is to win Negroes and their allies away from the Democratic Party as a whole and to organize them independently and in opposition to the two-party structure, in Mississippi as well as Michigan.

Revolution needed

The latter conclusion is the one that has been reached by some Negroes in Michigan and elsewhere after long and painful experience inside the Democratic Party. This opinion is shared by revolutionary socialists. It should be shared by everyone who understands that the winning of Negro equality requires revolution, not reform or gradualism, and that revolution requires new and independent political parties and institutions.

The situation in Mississippi is much more complex and difficult than in Michigan. Militant Mississippi Negroes are fighting to win the right to vote as well as to create a political instrument that can lead their struggle for freedom to victory. But the two things should not be mixed up. When we support the right to vote, we of course support the right to vote for and join any party one chooses,

---

Reprinted from the *Militant*, December 21, 1964

including the Democratic Party. But you don't have to vote for the Democrats merely because you have the right to. Voting for the Democrats and belonging to the Democratic Party, even the National Democratic Party, is not the road to Negro freedom. South or North. This point we will debate and defend with our last breath.

We don't know with any certainty what the Mississippi FDP's future course will be. We hope that it will be convinced, by its experience in 1964 and after, that the Democratic Party as a whole is hostile to the cause of Negro freedom, and that it will use its present organizational structure to build a progressive, independent alternative, state-wide and nationally, to the two parties historically and currently responsible for Negro oppression. When that happens, it will be as advanced politically as the FNP was in the recent Michigan campaign.

II

Another question that puzzled some readers of my report on the FNP's Nov. 3 vote was why I bothered to make a rough estimate of the FNP's percentage of the state-wide Negro vote (around 2 per cent) and not of its percentage of the total vote (much smaller, of course).

What is involved here was the FNP's implicit strategy in this election, which I was at fault in not explaining in my previous article.

The FNP and its candidates did not address themselves to all the voters. They spoke to and tried to reach and convince primarily the Negro voters. They thought that white voters, with few exceptions, would not understand or respond favorably to the idea of independent political action, black or white, in 1964. In any case, they felt that whatever resources, time and finances they had should be concentrated on their primary target, the Negro community.

Independent Force

This was in accord with their conviction that the *first* step was to unite the Negro people as an independent political force distinct from the major parties; and that everything else should be subordinated to that first step. They did not spell out what would happen after that. But they implied, more in their campaign speeches than in their literature, that once a substantial section of the Negro voters had rallied around the FNP and they had some independent political power to point to, *then* they would be in a position to deal with other forces ("negotiations from strength").

From this standpoint, the important thing in *this* election was not the FNP's percentage of the total state-wide vote but its percentage of the Negro vote (as the key link in the political chain).

It is unfortunate that the *National Guardian*'s correspondent could not understand the FNP's strategy and that *The Worker* chose to deliberately distort the FNP's concentration on Negro voters as "anti-white." One reason they were able to do this was that the FNP itself did not clarify this point sufficiently, resulting in a certain amount of demoralization among its own members after the strategy did not prove to be completely successful on election day.

III

A number of readers were surprised by my report that even the FNP's racial composition has not yet been settled definitively. This is understandable since from the start members of the FNP in Michigan and elsewhere have referred to it as "all-black."

But it has been a controversial point since the beginning. The practice is usually to have only Negro members, but not always, and the rule has never been written down in final constitutional form.

The original idea of the initiators of the FNP was that an all black membership was a way to exclude "unhealthy" white influences (by which some meant *all* white influences and others didn't); would alienate and discourage participation of conciliationist, "white-minded" Negroes, usually middle-class in orientation if not in composition; and make a strong appeal to the black masses, who are most suspicious of interracial organizations as a method whereby whites control from behind the scenes.

Other members were not so sure, but seemed most impressed by the last point (a strong way of winning the confidence of the black masses). They tended to hedge, however, that while they would want it all-black, this was not legally possible for any political party because of a Supreme Court decision doing away with racial restrictions on participation in primaries. This is really an evasion, however, because the FNP is a long way from the number of votes that would qualify it as a party legally required to hold primaries. There is nothing legal or constitutional preventing it from being all-black until then (a long enough period in which to formulate the program and knit together a tested leadership that could not really be deluded by any primary election practices or accidents). So why hasn't the FNP, among those groups presently existing, made a decision on this point one way or the other?

Partly out of uncertainty, I would say—an inability to motivate an all-black membership to others—to other Negroes, to white liberals, etc., and partly out of a desire to avoid unnecessary internal struggles. The question is strictly one of tactics (and not principles), to be decided strictly on the basis of whether an all-black or an inter-racial composition will best help to build the party. Sometimes it will be one type, sometimes another, depending on many objective and subjective conditions. It is possible to build Negro-controlled and Negro-led organizations either way. But whatever the decision is, it ought to be made without delay and clearly explained to both members and periphery. Otherwise the result is confusion, difficulty in recruiting, weakness of propaganda, etc.—unnecessary burdens for a party that is so hard to build without such added burdens.

If it's not to be all-black, that should be clarified as soon as possible, because many people will seize on this point to oppose an FNP (and have done so) when their *real and major* objection is to any new and independent political party controlled by Negroes (and not to the racial composition of such a party).

IV

I said above that we cannot be sure of how the Mississippi FDP will develop; the same should be stated for the Michigan FNP. Here I am concerned with correcting that part of my Nov. 13 report which said that "the party as a whole, far from being disheartened, is confidently facing the future and already preparing its next steps."

This statement was written at a time that the FNP appeared to have survived the first shock of its poor showing in the election and after a membership meeting where several ambitious new projects were brought up and passed in an atmosphere of enthusiasm.

Subsequently, however, it became clear that in reaction to the relatively low vote and as a result of some of the illusions and programmatic confusion I touched on in my previous article, a tendency arose favoring some kind of reconciliation with black liberalism. The proponents of this tendency put forward the need to "get back into the Negro mainstream" and "seek a coalition with other Negro forces" (meaning the Democratic Party). A decision along these lines would undoubtedly undermine or destroy the FNP's reason for existence as an independent party.

The initial reaction to the appearance of this tendency was one of demoralization. A number of the party's well known figures, including Rev. Albert B. Cleage, and many members have become inactive. Contrary to reports published locally, Cleage and his associates have not resigned from the FNP, but they do seem to be sitting back as the party enters its second internal crisis.

The picture of the FNP, therefore, does not seem as bright as when I wrote on Nov. 13, and its "main accomplishment"—the example of genuine political independence it set in the 1964 campaign—still needs to be strengthened and supplemented by a political and organizational program oriented to the long haul.

So the future of the FNP is not yet settled. The task of building an independent black party is harder than even its initiators anticipated.

SECTION IV. THE LOWNDES COUNTY FREEDOM ORGANIZATION

In early 1965, Blacks in Lowndes County, Alabama—who made up the vast majority of the population—began to organize themselves around issues such as voter registration and inadequate educational facilities. Out of these struggles there emerged in March 1966 the Lowndes County Freedom Organization with John Hullet as its chairman. Because of its symbol of a black panther, the organization also became known as the Black Panther Party, although there was no organizational relation between this group and the one that arose later in Oakland, California. From the beginning, the LCFO was aided by the Student Nonviolent Coordinating Committee, led by Stokely Carmichael, who had been working in Lowndes County since February 1965.

Deciding that the Democratic Party could not serve the interests of Blacks, the LCFO launched an electoral campaign to win control of the county offices in the November 1966 elections. Heading the ticket was Sidney Logan, the LCFO candidate for county sheriff. While achieving wide support from the Black population of Lowndes, the LCFO was fiercely denounced in the media and by a number of prominent Black leaders for its stated opposition to the Democratic and Republican parties.

Although the LCFO did not win the election, it did receive over 40 percent of the vote—a strong showing. After the election, it continued its efforts to organize the Black population under the name of the Lowndes County Freedom Party. However, in 1969 it abandoned its independent stance and merged with the National Democratic Party of Alabama. In 1970, John Hullet was elected Lowndes County sheriff on the Democratic Party ticket.

The articles in this section include two on-the-scene reports by Young Socialist Alliance leaders John Benson and Elizabeth Barnes; a speech by John Hullet given at a Los Angeles anti–Vietnam war rally on May 22, 1966; and an article by Barry Sheppard written shortly after the November 1966 elections, analyzing some aspects of the Lowndes County experience.

The Black Panther Party: A Report from Lowndes County
by John Benson

The southern freedom movement has taken a new step forward. In several Alabama black belt counties, where large numbers of Negroes will be voting for the first time this year, independent black parties are being formed in opposition to the Democratic Party. At least one, the Lowndes County Freedom Organization—known as the Black Panther Party because of its symbol—is strong enough to win in November if free elections are allowed.

The "liberal" Democratic Party candidates who are vying for the Negro vote in Alabama have been receiving extensive sympathetic coverage in the press. But the Black Panther Party has either been given the silent treatment or has borne the brunt of slanderous attacks.

The *New York Times* headed up the attack with an editorial on April 21, accusing the third party movement of "extremism for the sake of extremism," a "disruptive doctrine," and "a rule or ruin

---

Reprinted from the *Young Socialist*, May–June–July 1966

attitude." The *Times* directed its attack against the Student Nonviolent Coordinating Committee (SNCC) which has been active in building the independent parties. One week later the liberal *New York Post* attacked the Panther Party directly as "divisive" and "inflamatory."

What sends these editorialists into such a frenzy? Just the simple idea of Negroes organizing their own party to put their own candidates into office and openly campaigning against the Democratic Party.

I had just returned from Lowndes county when the attacks in the press began. I read that the Black Panther Party and SNCC were "disruptive," and that building a new party was "mischief making" and could "only produce frustration and defeat." But this was not a description of the movement I had seen.

What I saw in Lowndes is that the Negro people there are fed up with the racist officials. They are determined to end the killing and brutality and oppression they have been forced to live under every day of their lives. Contrary to the *New York Times*, I have never met people so united and enthusiastic about what they are doing. They are proud of their new party and go out of their way to explain what they are doing and why they are doing it. While in the county I attended the meetings of the new party and talked to its supporters and leaders. They explained to me how they began and developed their party and some of their plans for the future.

How the Black Panther Party was formed

The Negroes of Lowndes County have lived under one of the most blatantly racist administrations in the South. Even though they comprise eighty-one percent of the population, not a single Negro had been registered to vote before March of last year. At the same time, 2,500 whites are registered out of an eligible 1,900—*130 percent*! Sixty percent of all employed Negro men are farmers or farm laborers, most of them tenant farmers. Fifty percent of the Negro women employed are domestic workers.

While the median income for Negro families is $935, whites have a median income almost five times higher, and eighty-six white families own ninety percent of the land. Most of the officials in the county are members of these eighty-six families. As a result there is no money to pave the streets in the Negro areas and no money to build decent schools for Negro children.

The movement to change this situation began in January, 1965 with a discussion among several people about registering to vote. They held a meeting in the middle of February with fourteen people to discuss the registration forms and literacy test. Later that night one of the people, John Hullet, met a woman on his way home from work and told her about the meeting. She said she knew some people who wanted to register and together they arranged a meeting a few days later with eight more people.

By the next registration date, March 2, a total of thirty-eight people decided to go to the courthouse in Hayneville to register. Everyone was turned away and told to return two weeks later. When they came back only fourteen applications were processed and of these only two passed—a school teacher and John Hullet.

Before the second attempt to register, the Lowndes County Christian Movement for Human Rights was organized (known as the Christian Movement for short). Twenty-seven people attended the first meeting, including a representative from the Southern Christian Leadership Conference and one from SNCC. Only SNCC remained active in the county after that meeting.

Before beginning any major activities the new organization began a campaign to recruit new members. They held meetings every Sunday night in different areas of the county. In each area they recruited a person to canvass the area. After the first few meetings average attendance grew to 200–300.

After assembling a basic cadre, the Christian Movement began two projects—one to register Negroes to vote and the other to protest against inadequate schools. Most of the school protest activity was carried out by Lowndes County high school students. They began to protest within schools for better libraries, better dining room service, and an end to the practice of holding extra curricular activities during school hours.

During the summer, plans were made for a September school boycott with the aim of ousting the principal. The boycott was unsuccessful. But this experience along with a number of others made the people of Lowndes realize that protest against the white county government was not enough. Some began to think in terms of running the county government themselves.

Meanwhile voter registration was proceeding and discussions were beginning on who to vote for. Some people wanted to join the Democratic Party and work within it to elect Negro candidates. But the overwhelming majority saw the Democratic Party of Alabama as their most direct oppressor. A decision was made to see if it would be possible to organize a new party of their own and run candidates under their party's banner.

According to Alabama law, any political organization can hold a mass meeting on the day of the primary and the county registrar is required to put their candidates on the ballot for the November elections. Thus the Black Panther Party began to build itself with the aim of taking over the county courthouse in November 1966.

The Black Panther and the Democratic Party

From its inception the Black Panther Party has been organized in opposition to the Democratic Party. Their leaflet calling for the formation of a new party said,

> We all know what happened when the Mississippi Freedom Democratic Party tried to work within the structure of the national Democratic Party (the party of Lyndon Johnson, George Wallace, Bull Conner, James Clark, John Sparkman)—they got the door slammed in their faces.
>
> If Alabama doesn't want to repeat what happened in the Mississippi Freedom Democratic Party then Alabama doesn't have to.

This year the only offices the Black Panther is trying to win are the county sheriff, tax collector, coronor, tax assessor and board of education, as these are the officials the Negroes of Lowndes have to deal with every day. They are not concerned with which Democrat wins the statewide or federal offices. They believe that the only way to progress is to have their own party and this will take time and will have to be done in steps.

Opposition to 'liberals'

Despite their concentration on the Lowndes County elections, however, the supporters of the Black Panther Party are campaigning against the Democratic Party "liberals" who are running for state offices, and encouraging Negroes to vote only for Black Panther candidates. An article in the April 24 *New York Times* goes through a long list of southern "liberals" running in the Democratic primaries. With larger numbers of Negroes registered to vote, old style segregationists will more and more be challenged by northern style Democratic Party politicians. They may even let Negroes win a few more posts. This process has already begun in urban centers like Birmingham and Atlanta where Negroes have been registered for some time.

A campaign is being waged by the liberals and "moderate" Negro leadership to keep the Negro vote within the Democratic Party. It is focused on the governor's race where George Wallace who cannot legally succeed himself, is running for re-election through his wife, Lurleen Wallace. His major opponent is Attorney General Richmond Flowers, who has been presented as a courageous fighter for Negro rights.

This campaign is beginning to take on the phoney aspects of the Johnson-Goldwater campaign. Wallace is presented as the evil madman who is trying to circumvent the law and succeed himself while Flowers is the "friend of the Negro people." But Flowers is also a part of the racist administration of Alabama. His image is being refurbished just as Johnson, with the help of the press, changed his image from conservative Texan to liberal man of peace and civil rights fighter.

As Attorney General, Flowers was responsible for getting convictions on crimes against civil rights fighters, but he has never pressed for them. The people of Lowndes have had direct experience with his failures. When Jonathan Daniels, a white seminary student working on voter registration was killed in Lowndes, the killer went free.

Stokely Carmicheal, one of the main organizers of the new party, spoke on this at a meeting I attended:

> When Jonathan Daniels was killed, Richmond Flowers said he was for justice. He didn't say

he was for Negroes. He said he was for justice. When Sammy Younge was killed that cracker didn't say anything. When a white man is killed, he says he is for justice and when a Negro is killed, he doesn't say anything . . . He's only said he's for justice. He's never said he's for us, and there's a big difference.

King campaigning for Democratic Party

Martin Luther King and the Southern Christian Leadership Conference have entered the campaign directly in an attempt to stop the growth of a new, black party. King himself has toured Alabama urging people to vote for Flowers, but his tour, which went through the black belt counties, passed over Lowndes. From what I saw there his pro-Democratic party line would not be very well received.

Two Negro organizations, the Alabama Democratic Conference and the Confederation of Alabama's Political Organizations which was recently set up by SCLC's Hosea Williams, have endorsed Flowers for governor, and SCLC is backing Negroes in the Democratic primaries where they have no hope of winning.

Albert Turner, SCLC's Alabama project director and a candidate for state senator in the Democratic primary, showed up at a mass meeting in Perry County and attacked the Freedom Organization SNCC was trying to build there. He said, "SNCC doesn't register voters, doesn't care about registering voters," and pointed to two SNCC workers and said that all they wanted to do was split the Negro vote.

In spite of all these attacks, the Freedom Organizations in Alabama's black belt counties are gaining support. Pointing to the racism and oppression in the North, the organizers of the new parties argue that significant gains can best be won outside the framework of the Democratic Party.

Advocates of "reforming" the Democratic Party claim that increased Negro registration in Alabama has forced the Democratic Party to drop the words "white supremacy" from its state symbol—a white rooster. However, the actual credit for even this minor gain goes to the independent organization of the Negroes of Lowndes County. Not until the Freedom Organization had circulated a leaflet exposing this symbol did the Democratic Party replace this phrase with the word, "Democrat."

Although independent parties are being organized in a number of black belt counties, the Negroes of Lowndes realize that their's is the strongest. Whenever they are asked, people from Lowndes speak in other counties about their Freedom Organization. On one day alone, sixty people spoke in six different counties encouraging people to build new parties.

Frank Miles Jr., an officer of the Freedom Organization told me, "First, we're going to straighten out this county, then, we're going to spread abroad. First, we'll go into other counties of Alabama, then into the North, into Harlem, Chicago, and Watts."

There is no more powerful idea than the simple one that black people should organize themselves independently to do the things that the two major parties have failed to do for over a hundred years. But the Democratic Party and the ruling groups which use it to organize support for their interests will fight tooth and nail to keep Negroes voting Democratic. The Democratic Party is dependent on the Negro vote to win.

Stokely Carmicheal explained this in a talk when he said,

> The Democratic Party in this country is the most treacherous enemy the Negro has, period! Black people need power, and Bobby Kennedy doesn't want us to have power.
>
> It's in the interests of Robert Kennedy and Washington to squash the Lowndes County Freedom Organization because it will spread. And that's what we're working for—a national organization.

Every partisan of the Negro struggle should watch what happens in Lowndes County closely. As the *New York Times* articles show, the rulers of this country will also be watching it—doing everything within their power to prevent the Negroes of Lowndes from continuing their independent struggle in an effective way.

Any successes which the Black Panther has will encourage people throughout the country to follow its lead. Just the fact that the people in Lowndes have been able to organize the Black Panther Party is a gain in the struggle for Negro equality.

How the Black Panther Party Was Organized
by John Hullet

I'm happy to have the opportunity to come and share this evening with you. I'd like to give you a general idea of what's happening in the state of Alabama and in Lowndes County. This county, as far as I'm concerned, is one of the worst counties in the state of Alabama, and not only that, it is one of the poorest counties in the nation.

Lowndes County consists of a population of about 15,000 people. Out of these 15,000 people, 80 percent are Negroes, 20 percent white. The entire county is controlled entirely by whites. It has always been this way.

Last year in March, some 30 people assembled at the courthouse in Hayneville to make an attempt to get registered. They were talked about and many people were sitting by their radios that day, and their televisions, wanting to see what would happen in Lowndes County. We made the attempt and two weeks later, two people became registered voters. Today we have at least 2,500 registered Negro voters.

According to the 1960 statistics, there are only 1,900 possible white registered voters in the county. Today, all of these people are registered. Two years ago, 118 percent of these white people voted. In the general elections this year for governor, I learned that there will be even more white people voting.

Last year, we started a group in Lowndes County known as the Lowndes County Christian Movement for Human Rights. This was a civil rights group. We fought for integration in this county. We fought that Negroes might have a right to get registered to vote. We protested at the school so that all the people could have education—and for this we got nothing.

We sat down together and discussed our problems. We thought about what we were going to do with these 2,500 registered voters in the county, whether or not we were going to join Lyndon Baines Johnson's party. Then we thought about the other people in the state of Alabama who were working in this party. We thought of the city commissioner of Birmingham, Eugene Bull Conner; George Wallace who is now the governor of the state of Alabama; Al Lingo, who gave orders to those who beat the people when they got ready to make the march from Selma to Montgomery; the sheriff of Dallas County, known as Jim Clark—these people control the Democratic Party in the state of Alabama.

So the Negroes in Lowndes County decided that it's useless to stay in the Democratic Party or the Republican Party in the state of Alabama. Through the years, these are the people who kept Negroes from voting in the South and in the state of Alabama. Why join the Democratic Party?

A political group of our own

Some time ago, we organized a political group of our own known as the Lowndes County Freedom Organization, whose emblem is the Black Panther.

We were criticized, we were called communists, we were called everything else, black nationalists and what not, because we did this. Any group which starts at a time like this to speak out for what is right—they are going to be ridiculed. The people of Lowndes County realized this. Today we are moving further.

Too long Negroes have been begging, especially in the South, for things they should be working for. So the people in Lowndes County decided to organize themselves—to go out and work for the things we wanted in life—not only for the people in Lowndes County, but for every county in the state of Alabama, in the Southern states, and even in California.

You cannot become free in California while there are slaves in Lowndes County. And no person can be free while other people are still slaves, nobody.

In Lowndes County, there is a committee in the Democratic Party. This committee not only controls the courthouse, it controls the entire county. When they found out that the Negroes were going to run

Reprinted from *The Black Panther Party* (Merit Publishers, 1966)

candidates in the primary of the Democratic Party on May 3, they assembled themselves together and began to talk about what they were going to do. Knowing this is one of the poorest counties in the nation, what they decided to do was change the registration fees in the county.

Two years ago, if a person wanted to run for sheriff, tax collector or tax assessor, all he had to do was pay $50 and then he qualified to be the candidate. This year, the entrance fee is about $900. If a person wants to run, he has to pay $500 to run for office. In the primary, when they get through cheating and stealing, then the candidate is eliminated. So we decided that we wouldn't get into such a primary because we were tired of being tricked by the Southern whites. After forming our own political group today, we feel real strong. We feel that we are doing the right thing in Lowndes County.

We have listened to everybody who wanted to talk, we listened to them speak, but one thing we had to learn for ourselves. As a group of people, we must think for ourselves and act on our own accord. And this we have done.

Through the years, Negroes in the South have been going for the bones while whites have been going for the meat. The Negroes of Lowndes County today are tired of the bones—we are going to have some of the meat too.

Fighting the 'tricks' of the racists

At the present time, we have our own candidates which have been nominated by the Lowndes County Freedom Organization. And we fear that this might not be enough to avoid the tricks that are going to be used in Lowndes County against us.

In Lowndes County, the sheriff is the custodian of the courthouse. This is a liberal sheriff, too, who is "integrated," who walks around and pats you on the shoulder, who does not carry a gun. But at the same time, in the county where there are only 800 white men, there are 550 of them who walk around with a gun on them. They are deputies. This is true; it might sound like a fairy tale to most people, but this is true.

After talking to the sheriff about having the use of the courthouse lawn for our mass nominating meeting, not the courthouse but just the lawn, he refused to give the Negroes permission. We reminded him that last year in August, that one of the biggest Klan rallies that has ever been held in the state of Alabama was held on this lawn of this courthouse. And he gave them permission. A few weeks ago an individual who was campaigning for governor—he got permission to use it. He used all types of loud speakers and anything that he wanted.

But he would not permit Negroes to have the use of the courthouse. For one thing he realized that we would build a party—and if he could keep us from forming our own political group then we would always stand at the feet of the Southern whites and of the Democratic Party. So we told him that we were going to have this meeting, we were going to have it here, on the courthouse lawn. And we wouldn't let anybody scare us off. We told him, we won't expect you to protect us, and if you don't, Negroes will protect themselves.

Then we asked him a second time to be sure he understood what we were saying. We repeated it to him the second time. And then we said to him, sheriff, if you come out against the people, then we are going to arrest you.

And he said, I will not give you permission to have this meeting here. I can't protect you from the community.

Then we reminded him that according to the law of the state of Alabama, that this mass meeting which was set up to nominate our candidates must be held in or around a voters' polling place. And if we decide to hold it a half a mile away from the courthouse, some individual would come up and protest our mass meeting. And our election would be thrown out.

So we wrote the Justice Department and told them what was going to happen in Lowndes County.

All of a sudden the Justice Department started coming in fast into the county. They said to me, John, what is going to happen next Tuesday at the courthouse?

I said, We are going to have our mass meeting. And he wanted to know where. And I said on the lawn of the courthouse.

He said, I thought the sheriff had told you you couldn't come there. And I said, Yes, but we are going to be there.

Then he wanted to know, if shooting takes place, what are we going to do. And I said, that we are going to stay out here and everybody die together.

And then he began to get worried, and I said, Don't worry. You're going to have to be here to see it out and there's no place to hide, so whatever happens, you can be a part of it.

And then he began to really panic. And he said, There's nothing I can do.

And I said, I'm not asking you to do anything. All I want you to know is we are going to have a mass meeting. If the sheriff cannot protect us, then we are going to protect ourselves. And I said to him, through the years in the South, Negroes have never had any protection, and today we aren't looking to anybody to protect us. We are going to protect ourselves.

That was on Saturday. On Sunday, at about 2 o'clock, we were having a meeting, and we decided among ourselves that we were going to start collecting petitions for our candidates to be sure that they got on the ballot. The state laws require at least 25 signatures of qualified electors and so we decided to get at least 100 for fear somebody might come up and find fault. And we decided to still have our mass meeting and nominate our candidates.

About 2:30, here comes the Justice Department again, and he was really worried. And he said he wasn't satisfied. He said to me, John, I've done all I can do, and I don't know what else I can do, and now it looks like you'll have to call this meeting off at the courthouse.

And I said, we're going to have it.

He stayed around for awhile and then got in his car and drove off, saying, I'll see you tomorrow, maybe. And we stayed at this meeting from 2:30 until about 11:30 that night. About 11:15, the Justice Department came walking up the aisle of the church and said to me, Listen. I've talked to the Attorney General of the state of Alabama, and he said that you can go ahead and have a mass meeting at the church and it will be legal.

Then we asked him, Do you have any papers that say that's true, that are signed by the Governor or the Attorney General? And he said no. And we said to him, Go back and get it legalized, and bring it back here to us and we will accept it.

And sure enough, on Monday at 3 o'clock, I went to the courthouse and there in the sheriffs office were the papers all legalized and fixed up, saying that we could go to the church to have our mass meeting.

To me, this showed strength. When people are together, they can do a lot of things, but when you are alone you cannot do anything.

There are 600 Negroes in the county who did not trust in themselves and who joined the Democratic Party. We warned the entire state of Alabama that running on the Democratic ticket could not do them any good, because this party is controlled by people like Wallace; and whoever won would have to do what these people said to do.

Now, to me, the Democratic Party primaries and the Democratic Party is something like an integrated gambler who carries a card around in his pocket and every now and then he has to let somebody win to keep the game going. To me, this is what the Democratic Party means to the people in Alabama. It's a gambling game. And somebody's got to win to keep the game going every now and then.

There is another guy who was running on the ticket calling himself a liberal, the Attorney General of the state of Alabama, Richmond Flowers. Most of you have heard about him. When he started campaigning to the people of Alabama, especially the Negro people, he assembled all their leaders and he made all kinds of promises to them—if you elect me for your governor, I'll do everything in the world for you.

And at the same time, he never made a decent campaign speech to the white people of this state. We kept warning our people in the state of Alabama that this was a trick and many Negroes listened to their so-called leaders, who profess to speak for the state of Alabama, and they got caught in the trap too.

I would like to say here, and this is one thing I am proud of, the people in Lowndes County stood together, and the 600 people who voted in the Democratic primary have realized one thing, that they were tricked by the Democratic Party. And now they too are ready to join us with the Lowndes County Freedom Organization whose emblem is the black panther.

We have seven people who are running for office this year in our county; namely, the coronor, three members of the board of education—and if we win those three, we will control the board of education—tax collector, tax assessor, and the individual who carries a gun at his side, the sheriff.

Let me say this—that a lot of persons tonight asked me, Do you really think if you win that you will be able to take it all over, and live?

I say to the people here tonight—yes, we're going to do it. If we have to do like the present sheriff, if we have to deputize every man in Lowndes County 21 and over, to protect people, we're going to do it.

There was something in Alabama a few months ago they called fear. Negroes were afraid to move on their own, they waited until the man, the people whose place they lived on, told them they could get registered. They told many people, don't you move until I tell you to move and when I give you an order, don't you go down and get registered. . . .

Evictions and threats

Then all the people were being evicted at the same time and even today in Lowndes County, there are at least 75 families that have been evicted, some now are living in tents while some are living in one-room houses—with 8 or 9 in a family. Others have split their families up and are living together with their relatives or their friends. But they are determined to stay in Lowndes County, until justice rolls down like water.

Evicting the families wasn't all—there were other people who live on their own places who owe large debts, so they decided to foreclose on these debts to run Negroes off the place. People made threats—but we're going to stay there, we aren't going anywhere.

I would like to let the people here tonight know why we chose this black panther as our emblem. Many people have been asking this question for a long time. Our political group is open to whoever wants to come in, who would like to work with us. But we aren't begging anyone to come in. It's open, you come, at your own free will and accord.

But this black panther is a vicious animal as you know. He never bothers anything, but when you start pushing him, he moves backwards, backwards, and backwards into his corner, and then he comes out to destroy everything that's before him.

Negroes in Lowndes County have been pushed back through the years. We have been deprived of our rights to speak, to move, and to do whatever we want to do at all times. And now we are going to start moving. On November 8 of this year, we plan to take over the courthouse in Hayneville. And whatever it takes to do it, we're going to do it.

We've decided to stop begging. We've decided to stop asking for integration. Once we control the courthouse, once we control the board of education, we can build our school system where our boys and girls can get an education in Lowndes County. There are 89 prominent families in this county who own 90 percent of the land. These people will be taxed. And we will collect these taxes. And if they don't pay them, we'll take their property and sell it to whoever wants to buy it. And we know there will be people who will buy land where at the present time they cannot buy it. This is what it's going to take.

We aren't asking any longer for protection—we won't need it—or for anyone to come from the outside to speak for us, because we're going to speak for ourselves now and from now on. And I think not only in Lowndes County, not only in the state of Alabama, not only in the South, but in the North—I hope they too will start thinking for themselves. And that they will move and join us in this fight for freedom. Thank you and good night.

What I Saw in Lowndes County, Alabama
by Elizabeth Barnes

HAYNEVILLE, Ala.—The black people of Lowndes County, Ala., have taken seriously the idea of black power and are organizing a political party independent of the Democrats and Republicans. This party, the Lowndes County Freedom Organization (also known as the Black Panther Party because of its ballot symbol), is running its candidates in the next general election with the object of taking over the county.

Before my visit to Lowndes County, I had heard the story of the Lowndes County Freedom Organization and knew about the ideas of the leadership. What my trip showed me was that the people in Lowndes not only have good ideas, but they know how to put these ideas into practice. A lot can be learned by watching the leaders of the Lowndes County Freedom Organization as they go about their work. They are real mass leaders who are organizing the black people there to rely on themselves.

I found that many of the leaders and activists in the Lowndes County Freedom Organization have gained experience in other working-class struggles. Many are veterans of the trade union movement. Others played key roles in the Montgomery bus boycott of 1956. Most of the men who are activists in the Freedom Organization, like most of the black men in Lowndes County, are workers in heavy labor occupations in the building trades. The majority of them go into nearby Montgomery for work.

The leaders of the Freedom Organization are all from Lowndes County. There is a thin layer of middle-class Negroes who live in Lowndes, but they are not leaders in the Freedom Organization. The leaders are working people who have roots in the community. They have suffered the same things that the masses of black people in Lowndes have been suffering for years—inadequate housing, schools, food and clothes. They know what the problems are, and they know how to go about changing things.

Reprinted from the *Militant*, July 25, 1966

The median income for Negro families is $935. What this means is that the homes are run down and unpainted, with collapsing porches and not enough room inside. It means little furniture and four or five children in a bed. It means few windows and fewer glass windows. It means getting all your water for cooking and bathing from an outside pump and using outside toilets.

The children go to broken down one-room schools with inadequate supplies and inferior instruction. Mrs. R.L. Strickland, who is running as Freedom Organization candidate for the board of education, told me that the children have to take up school time in the winter to gather wood to heat the school buildings. Their school buses are unheated and often break down because they are in bad repair. Mrs. Strickland said that one night when her small children did not arrive home from school, she and her husband found them abandoned in the dark in a school bus which had broken down.

Eighty-six white families own 90 percent of the county's land. Much of this is rented out to Negroes to farm. But the number of Negro families supporting themselves by farming is declining because the price of cash crops is going down due to the growing mechanization of farming. Many of the women farm while their husbands work, to supplement the income. From their farm work, they usually get several hundred dollars a year. Most of the Negro farms have to use draft animals.

The people in the Freedom Organization have one belief which is key to everything they are doing. That is the idea that "if we want to make progress, we must rely on ourselves." This became apparent to me when I went with John Hulett, chairman of the Lowndes County Freedom Organization, to visit homes in the county, organizing people to register. At that time, the Mississippi march had just been completed. Mr. Hulett explained to the people that on the Mississippi march, outside people had gone into communities to help register voters. He told them that in Lowndes, "We are registering the people ourselves." He said, "Then, we won't need any marchers through here."

Having been on the last leg of the march, I was able to contrast the voter registration done on the march with that being done in Lowndes. On the march, the people in the communities showed a distrust toward those who wanted them to register. Often they would say that they had registered when they had not.

In Lowndes, the overwhelming majority of the Negroes worked with John Hulett to get as many people registered as possible. More important, they are motivated to register because they have their own party to vote for in the fall—a party that provides a real alternative to the racists.

Registration work is considered the primary task of the Freedom Organization at this time. Mr. Hulett estimated that thus far, 2,600 Negroes have been registered in the county. He explained that 2,200 whites are registered—a figure greater than the number of whites over 21 that live in the county. Some of them are even believed to be dead people. The Freedom Organization intends to investigate and challenge some of these white names.

One of the prime tasks of the Freedom Organization is to politically educate its members. The leaders of the Freedom Organization believe only if the masses of people understand the reality of their situation, can they play a meaningful role in the organization.

Education is carried on in many different ways. Freedom Organization leaders and activists are continually canvassing the community, going house to house, talking to people about what they are trying to do. Besides this, there are frequent meetings of the Freedom Organization held in the various communities. (Lowndes County is divided into 21 communities.) Here the candidates speak and political questions are discussed. These meetings usually attract from 175 to 200 people.

In addition to the Freedom Organization, there is an organization in Lowndes called the Lowndes County Christian Movement. The Christian Movement is a broader organization than the Freedom Organization. Anyone may belong whether they support the Freedom Organization or not. Most of the activists do support the Freedom Organization and its candidates, and there is overlapping leadership between the two organizations. Once a week, the Lowndes County Christian Movement has a meeting in each community. People are less hesitant about coming to the smaller community meetings held by the Christian Movement than to the Freedom Organization, and these meetings often become a stepping stone to the Freedom Organization itself.

As he canvassed the community, Mr. Hulett encouraged people to come to the community meetings, reminding them of the time and place. He told them that they could bring up any topics that they wanted to discuss.

At the community meetings, someone from the community is chairman. At a meeting in Moses Community I attended, they discussed plans for building a playground, a library, outhouses for the church and the purchase of an icebox for the school to keep the children's milk from souring. Many of these projects were already well-launched with committees working on them. An announcement was made at the meeting that voting machines would be brought to a future meeting so that people could learn how to use them.

There were about 35 to 40 people present at the meeting, including children. Most of the adults participated in some way—by giving suggestions or by volunteering to work on committees.

Importance of organization

At the meeting, a collection was taken which came to $37. This represented big sacrifices for the people there. Both the Freedom Organization and the Christian Movement rely on their members to supply the funds to keep the organization going and most of the money is collected at meetings such as this one.

To the people in Lowndes, it is the Freedom Organization which is important—not any particular leader or candidate. They do not rely on any one person to make decisions, but on the team of people that make up the broad leadership of the organization, and ultimately on themselves. Mr. Hulett explains this to people as he visits them. He says that the Freedom Organization builds a fence around its candidates—and that the candidates must do what the organization wants them to.

There are frequent executive committee meetings, where things are discussed and the decisions are made. The leadership knows what the people in the organization want, and it is responsible to carry that out. That does not mean that the leaders do not feel responsible for trying to be sure that the right decisions are made. The leaders argue for their point of view, just like everyone else.

The leaders of the Freedom Organization see the elections as an important test for the organization. But they realize that there are tremendous obstacles in the way of reaching their goal of electing their candidates, and they understand if they are unable to do this, it will not mean that the organization has failed or that it was wrong to build it. They realize that the struggle is a hard and long one, and that victory cannot be won overnight. They are prepared to protect themselves against terror, fraud and any contingency. They also realize that this is the first time the black people of Lowndes will have voted and that there will be some fear.

In addition to these problems, there are the Uncle Toms. At one of the community meetings, someone spoke against a certain retired teacher who was "running his mouth off" about the Freedom Organization. It seems that the white community was putting up this teacher as the "leader" to tell the black people how to vote and whom to vote for, despite the fact that he had never been active in the struggle.

The people in Lowndes County feel they are building something for future generations. As he visited the homes of the people, Mr. Hulett would often point to the children and say, "Think of these children here, of their future. Do you want them to get the kind of education that you and I got?"

At an executive board meeting of the Lowndes County Christian Movement, the chairman, Charles Smith, explained that it would take a long time to achieve what they wanted; probably the balance of their lives. The work has only begun, he said. The white man is very tricky.

The activists in the Freedom Organization work hard. They see all this effort as worthwhile in winning a better life for their children—and for black people around the country, as well. They see their organization as an example for others to follow. As Mr. Hulett told many of those he visited, "We want to show right here in Lowndes County that it is possible to build a clean political organization."

A meeting in Blackbelt Community was ended with Hulett pointing out that Johnson and Wallace were essentially the same. Johnson didn't do anything about the tear-gassing of the marchers, he pointed out.

Although the Freedom Organization has deep roots in Lowndes County, it is isolated from the rest of the country by the fact that there are no other such organizations nationally independent of the Republicans and Democrats with which it can link up. There have been attempts in three other black-belt counties, thus far, to set up freedom organizations, but these have not gotten off the ground yet.

The fact that they have carried through their struggle on their own, while others have failed, is a tribute to the leadership in Lowndes County. Others around the country would do well to learn more about how they did it, and to follow their example.

Black Power and the Democrats

by Barry Sheppard

What next for the black power movement? A recent conference of the staff of the Student Nonviolent Coordinating Committee began to grapple with this question, according to a report by Andrew Kopkind in the Jan. 7 *New Republic*. Kopkind has been one of the relatively few writers in the liberal press to give perceptive and generally sympathetic coverage of the black power movement.

Kopkind says that "the conference came to a number of tentative conclusions that establish a

Reprinted from the *Militant*, January 23, 1967

direction for black radical energies over the next years.

> First of all, focus of new activities will definitely swing to Northern urban areas from the rural South. As SNCC sees it, the failure of the Lowndes County Freedom Organization (the 'Black Panther Party') and the Mississippi Freedom Democrats to take power is not so much a function of bad organizing as it is of isolation. 'The place that really has the power is the North,' Carmichael said . . .
>
> In Northern cities (and perhaps some urbanized areas of the South, which behave like Northern ghettos), SNCC wants to start 'Freedom Organizations,' with their own political, educational, economic, and cultural components. That may mean third political parties, co-op businesses, freedom schools, and 'Afro' cultural centers.

SNCC helped to organize the Lowndes County Freedom Party, as it is now called, which ran a slate of candidates for local offices in Lowndes County, Ala. in the November elections. The new, independent, black-led party received 41 percent of the vote, which was enough to establish the organization as a legal party but, of course, fell short of winning the election and taking over the county.

Background of election

Negroes are a majority in Lowndes. Why didn't they win? A full report on the election was printed in *The Militant* of Nov. 21, but briefly, this is the background:

Two years ago, there were only a handful of Negroes registered in Lowndes. The county was known for violence against Negroes and civil rights workers (Mrs. Liuzzo was murdered there during the Selma-Montgomery march in 1965). White control of the county, in spite of the fact that whites were a 20 percent minority, was ensured by white control of the Democratic Party and the county government.

The Lowndes County Freedom Organization got its start in 1965, with help from Stokely Carmichael and others from SNCC. In spite of the fact that Lowndes is mostly rural with a scattered population, and the Negroes there are very poor, not even possessing telephones, a strong organization with a strong local leadership was constructed. Successfully overcoming fear and old habits of thought, the LCFO helped register something over 2,600 Negroes by September of last year.

During the primary elections last May, the new party nominated its own candidates at a mass meeting of 900 Negroes. To do this, it had to educate the newly-registered black people of Lowndes about the need for an independent party of their own. They could not both vote in the Democratic primary and vote to nominate the Black Panther candidates. During the primary electioneering, Rev. Martin Luther King campaigned in Alabama for Negroes to vote for Attorney General Flowers, as against Mrs. Wallace in the Democratic primary, placing an additional hurdle in the path of the new party.

By the time of the November elections, the LCFO was able to increase its support to 1,600, the number of votes its main candidate received. It did this in spite of the fact that it represented a pioneering effort, without significant support from similar parties elsewhere in the country. It had to contend with threats of violence and some actual violence at the polls. Some white plantation owners were able to intimidate Negroes working on their land into voting Democratic. There were instances of white fraud at the polls.

Significant step

Against all these obstacles, the fact that the new party won 41 percent of the vote and established itself as a legal party is a tremendous achievement and represents an important victory. Whether the new party will be able to continue in the face of all the forces arrayed against it remains to be seen. If their past record is any indication, the Negroes of Lowndes will be seriously challenging the Democratic Party in the 1968 elections. In any case, the Black Panther has already provided an example for the whole Negro struggle.

The Black Panther Party has certainly been no "failure." Its major problem, as is indicated by the SNCC discussion, it its isolation. The idea of organizing in the big city ghettos, which Kopkind reports is SNCC's orientation, points the way out of that isolation.

But there still remains a lack of clarity in SNCC

and in the black power movement generally about exactly what kind of organizing should be done in the ghettos. This lack of clarity revolves around the question of the Democratic Party.

MFDP position

The Mississippi Freedom Democratic Party, for example, put up independent candidates in the last election against Mississippi Democrats. But the MFDP considers itself part of the national Democratic Party. At least, that is how it defined itself in 1964, when it supported Johnson—and it has never publicly modified that stand.

In 1964, the MFDP's position was that the main enemy is the Southern racists in the Democratic Party, and not the national Democratic Party. This is an important issue, bearing directly upon the kind of political action SNCC intends to try to carry out in the ghettos. Should independent parties, or a national single independent black party, be built, or should the policy of supporting the Democratic Party or one wing of it be maintained?

The answer to this question can be found not only in analyzing the nature of the Democratic Party, but also in the concrete results of coalitionism to date. For the past 30 years or so, Negro leaders have generally supported the Democratic Party, and Negroes have voted Democratic in their majority. What are the results of this policy?

The facts of the matter are that Negroes are worse off in relation to whites now than they were 10 years ago. The gap between white and black has increased. Those gains which have been won, have not come as a result of supporting the Democrats, but as a result of independent action such as street demonstrations. Thirty years of supporting the Democrats has not brought the end of the oppression of the Negro people any closer.

The facts of life in Harlem, Watts, Chicago's West Side, etc. are eloquent testimony to the failure of the policy of coalitionism with the Democratic Party.

Both the Democratic and Republican parties are dedicated to preserving the racist capitalist system at home and abroad. They are run by capitalist politicians whose first loyalty is to the rich who profit from racism. These politicians will pay lip service to equality when they think it will get them votes, but will never make the fundamental changes necessary to change the system and end racism.

These capitalist parties are not controlled by the black people, or by most of the whites in spite of the fact that most people vote for them. They are political instruments designed to keep black people and other working people in their place, and promote the interests of the rich.

To make any real gains, black people are going to have to win some *power*, black political power. This can't be done by electing individual black Democrats or Republicans, because those individuals do not represent the black community but are beholden to the political machines controlled by the white capitalist rulers. Real black power, a fair share of political power for Negroes, can only be won through independent black political action against the racist parties of big business. Black people have to have their own political instrument, their own political party controlled by them, to win any measure of black power.

Is the proposal to organize an independent black party on a national scale feasible?

The strategic basis for such a party already exists. It was created by the capitalist system of segregation, which has herded millions of black people together in the ghettos of the biggest cities of the North and South. As whites continue to flee from the big cities to the suburbs, the relative weight of the blacks becomes ever greater. Right now, if the black people were united in a party of their own, they are so situated that they could sweep the elections in dozens of congressional districts and Southern counties where they are a majority. A black party could elect a bloc of candidates that could even hold the legislative balance of power in Washington and several big industrial states, and therefore be able to force some serious concessions from the capitalist parties.

Wide impact

Because Negroes are only 10 or 11 percent of the population, a black party could not expect to win national power by itself. But the creation of a black party would have a profound impact on the whole political structure of the nation, not just in the ghettos.

The withdrawal of Negroes into a party of their

own would signal the doom of the Democratic Party as a major national party. Deprived of the black vote, the Democrats would be unable to win elections in the key Northern states.

That's not all. A break of the Negroes from the capitalist parties, which today means a break from the Democratic Party, would provoke an acute crisis in the labor movement, whose leaders now serve as junior partners of the Democrats. With Negroes abandoning the party, with the relative weight of the Dixiecrats increasing inside the party, and with the Democrats unable to win national elections, the union movement's coalition with the Democrats would be plainly seen by everybody for what it actually is—bankrupt as well as stupid.

Dissatisfaction with being a tail to the Democratic donkey, which already exists in labor's ranks, would accelerate tremendously. Sentiment for an independent labor party, already being generated by other factors, would come to a boil. The decline of the Democratic Party would hasten the formation of a labor party.

Right from the start a labor party would be compelled, in everything it did and said, to take the existence of a Negro party into account. It would most likely seek an alliance between the two parties, which could only be done by adopting the just demands of the Negro people. On their side, the Negroes, when assured that an alliance would not subordinate their interests or sidetrack the struggle for equality, would probably welcome the cooperation with a labor party. The result would eventually be either a merger of the two parties or their close collaboration in a struggle for political power. What began as the independent action of a minority could end as the reconstruction of society by a majority.

Organizing an independent black political party is not easy, North or South. There are many difficulties to be overcome, the chief of which is the relentless opposition of most of the Negro leaders, who are wedded to coalitionism with the Democrats. But the example of Lowndes shows that this, too, can be overcome with the proper leadership.

SECTION V. THE CASE FOR AN INDEPENDENT BLACK PARTY

The most dynamic demand among Afro-Americans today is for black power. Although they are the biggest minority in this country, numbering 22 million people or over 11 per cent of the population, making up about 20 per cent of the work force, and due to become the majority in ten of the larger Northern cities by the 1970s, black Americans have been permitted little power of any kind, economic, social, cultural or political. The denial of real or proportional political representation to such a key sector is one of the most glaring injustices of this capitalist society.

How has the racist ruling class managed to keep black people in such a politically powerless state? How can this condition be overcome? This is one of the most pressing problems facing black Americans—and their future depends upon finding the correct solution to it.

To the extent that black people have participated in politics to date, it has been almost entirely through the two big capitalist parties, the Democrats and Republicans, that is within terms laid down by the representatives of their oppressors and exploiters. The main reason for the meager results achieved after 13 years of struggle since the 1954 Supreme Court decision has been their dependence upon the two capitalist parties which have conceded little but a series of phony "civil rights" bills.

The lack of any substantial gains through this avenue underscores the need for organizing and exercising genuinely independent black political power. Here are some of the reasons why this kind of political action can bring considerable benefits to the black masses, give maximum leverage to their united power, and prepare them for the tasks of revolutionizing this oppressive racist capitalist society.

Why an independent black party is needed

The black people's lack of political power is so serious because politics is the key to breaking out of the vicious circle of social, economic and cultural deprivation and discrimination imposed on them by this system. It is not something far away from their everyday lives or divorced from their basic needs. Political power means the capacity to assert the needs and aspirations of a group and to see that they are fulfilled. Full political power means that a group runs its own affairs and determines its own destiny. Even the possession of some measure of political power means that the group has a voice in deciding the terms of its existence.

In the United States today black people are effectively excluded from all the crucial decisions affecting their fate. The policies that determine how they will live are made by others and imposed upon them. Every aspect of Afro-American life is governed by the decisions of the Democratic and Republican agents of the capitalist rulers of this country. Their actions (or inactions) perpetuate inequality, poverty, degradation, police brutality, insecurity, unemployment, low-paying jobs, bad schools, inadequate housing and medical facilities, a shorter life-span and all the other evils suffered by black Americans.

These intolerable conditions cannot be fundamentally changed except through a massive, united, all-out fight that hits the Big Business rulers at the center of their grip. This is their control of legal authority and state power. But in order to carry out an effective fight for black political power, Afro-Americans must have their own organization under their own control.

The masters of this country understand the

"The Case for an Independent Black Party" was a resolution adopted by the Socialist Workers Party at its Twenty-second National Convention in October 1967.

need for political action that benefits them and for political organizations that serve them. That is why they have political parties—not just one, but two—which they control and through which they exercise a political monopoly.

Of course, it is not only through such parties that they maintain their rule. They have the ownership of industry, the power of money and credit, control of the mass media and schools, and ultimately the police and armed forces. But their power does not come out of the barrel of the gun alone. If they relied solely on naked force, the resources of their rulership would soon be exhausted by an incessant battle between the oppressors and the oppressed. Like other master classes throughout history, our own rulers practice deception to make their power and misrule seem legitimate and induce the subjugated and exploited classes to accept it without resistance.

The two-party shell game, and especially the portrayal of the Democratic Party as a party of the people, is an important part of this deception. While the role of this party in upholding and enforcing racism is clear in the South, it wears the mask of liberalism in the North. But in practice it is no less racist than the Republican Party there. Under duress it throws black people a few concessions, a few posts, a few tokens to placate them though it has no intention of ending racism. The two-party setup fosters the illusion that black people will get freedom through gradual reform of capitalism and its institutions. The history of the past hundred years testifies that this is a lie. Black people will never be liberated by supporting political parties that are controlled by their oppressors and that are so constructed and operated that they will always be controlled by their oppressors.

Big Business and the racist system it preserves for its own profit cannot be challenged for control of legitimate authority so long as voters are restricted to choosing between the candidates and programs of the two parties under their thumb. However, the tradition of electoral democracy which the rich manipulate for their own ends is potentially a gun which can be loaded against them. It claims to permit people the right to establish their own political parties which can take over and run local, state or national government. Thus a black party independent of capitalist control could take advantage of this right to gain control of some areas of government. If the capitalists tried to prevent this, that would expose the farce of their electoral democracy and create conditions where the masses could legitimately fight "by any means necessary" for freedom against the tyranny of the very rich white minority—a far smaller minority than the millions of black people.

If it is to move ahead, the black liberation movement must be able to counter the enormous facilities for political deception used by its enemy. The 1964 campaign provided convincing evidence of the hold the treacherous two-party system has over black voters. No group in the country supported the presidential ticket of the Democratic Party in greater proportion than the black voters (almost 95 per cent). What did they get in return? A civil rights law in 1965 that is largely unenforced, a civil rights bill in 1966 that was filibustered to death, a penny-ante "war on poverty" that leaves 90 per cent of the black people as poor as they ever were, housing and schooling that are more segregated then they were in 1964.

The ouster of Adam Clayton Powell from his congressional seat is one more proof of the tricksterism of the Democratic Party. Many black people looked upon Powell as a representative spokesman who had acquired a position of considerable influence on the summits of power in Washington. But he was only a lieutenant, a tool of the Democratic machine which neither he nor his black supporters controlled in any respect. So the real powers could easily get rid of him once they felt he no longer served a useful purpose.

The same is true about the others who work in the two capitalist parties and occupy decorative posts in them or at their mercy. While they get personal advantages and honors from these positions, that does not change the conditions of the black masses. How much good does the appointment of a black Supreme Court Justice do if the entire local, state and federal legal system is stacked against justice for the Afro-American?

The real face, and not the hypocritical mask, of the Democratic Party can be seen in its "white backlash" aspect which has come more into the open since 1964. Ex-governor Wallace of Alabama is preparing a nationwide bid for the presidency while still a ranking Democrat. And Johnson's vice president, Hubert Humphrey, publicly embraces the notorious Georgia racist, Democratic Governor Lester Maddox.

The notion that the Democratic Party (or its Republican duplicate) can be reformed from a party of racism into a party of liberation is wishful thinking to the point of fantasy. As Malcolm X said, a chicken is not constructed to produce a duck egg; similarly, a capitalist party is not constructed to produce freedom for Afro-Americans. The Democratic Party is capable of giving concessions, especially to certain middleclass elements whom the capitalists expect to use to contain and police the black masses. But it is incapable of promoting and making the profound economic and political changes needed to solve the problems of millions of oppressed. Black people who think they are going to "take over" part of the Democratic organization and "use" it in the interests of the black masses are fooling themselves or the masses; they themselves are the ones who get taken over and used.

Equally futile is the concept of a "third force" advanced by some black power advocates and by Adam Clayton Powell. According to this proposal, black Democrats, black Republicans and black independents should get together politically, bargain as a united bloc with the two capitalist parties, and deliver or withhold the votes they influence depending on which one offered the best bargain. Although this is called "independent political action," it is nothing of the kind. It is a spurious substitute because it would leave black voters dependent on the promises of two racist parties, rather than of one.

At most, it could bring a few more concessions rather than any fundamental changes. And it cannot even bring many concessions because it overlooks the fact that the two capitalist parties are controlled by the same forces, to whom it does not much matter whether black people vote Democratic or Republican. Just so long as that is their only choice, just so long as there is no alternative to the two parties they control, the ruling powers have the black voters at their mercy.

The only way that black people can get out of the Democratic fire without falling into the Republican frying pan is to establish their own party. They must do this because neither major party is free of capitalist control. In most large industrial countries there are labor and other non-capitalist parties based on the working people and their organizations. If such a party existed here, black people might find a real alternative in joining and supporting it.

But organized labor in the United States missed its chances in the 1930s and again in the late 1940s to cut loose from the Democratic Party and create its own party with the perspective of taking political power away from the capitalists and establishing a government of the workers and their allies. Just as Uncle Toms have failed to lead black people onto an independent road, so too at critical junctures in the past, union bureaucrats have prevented the American workers from forming their own party. An independent mass party of the workers will eventually be formed here as elsewhere. But it will not arise until the workers become radicalized and able to defeat and replace their present capitalist-minded misleaders.

Black people cannot wait until that happens—they need political weapons now. Whatever allies they may get in the future, they have no alternative now but to build a political party of their own.

Some ultra-lefts who are deeply disillusioned with the two major parties (or even certain radical parties) reject all political action as useless or diversionary. They mistakenly identify politics with narrow electoral activity or vote-catching. They fail to understand what politics really is or can be and what a powerful impetus an independent black party could give to the revolutionary movement.

There are different, and even opposite, kinds of politics. What Americans see all around them, and what usually passes for politics, is the phony, status quo politics of the racists and shysters, the horse-trading and hypocrisy of the Democrats and Republicans in which a few get rich at the expense of the many.

But there can be another type of politics. When black people get together and fight for control of the schools in their community, that is political action. When black people come out into the streets, pushed beyond endurance by racist cops, gouging merchants and landlords and all the other miseries of ghetto life, that too is a kind of politics.

The trouble with these attempts to change the policies that affect ghetto life is that they are limited, sporadic, unorganized, semi-conscious and unsustained. If such mass actions and direct struggles were combined with a consistently organized struggle to gain political power, if they were initiated and led by a political party that rightly claimed to speak and act for the struggling masses, this would be much more than a vote-catching device or an electoral doublecross.

Electoral activity need not be the opposite of revolutionary struggle; it has been and can be an essential spur to it. It can be a valuable part of the arsenal of struggle techniques in a war where every means necessary must be employed.

History has known political parties that combined running candidates for office with mass struggles under their leadership to abolish oppressive social systems. Lenin's Bolsheviks are the best-known example.

A political party based on the ghetto could carry out many worthwhile activities in addition to running for or holding political offices. It could conduct education about black history and revolutionary struggles elsewhere; take measures to form cooperatives and credit systems to ease the economic squeeze; defend black victims of government persecution; initiate literary campaigns among adults; organize Afro-American cultural affairs and community recreation. Its contests for or control of legitimate authority would give it much more leverage in fights against landlords, brutal cops, and job discrimination. It could organize neighborhood patrols against crime and rackets and demand an end to the alien and repressive police powers of racist rulers. It could provide a broad framework for unifying various black groups in common struggle.

It will take more than spontaneous eruptions to win black liberation; it will require an organized, sustained, long-term fight. If a black party starts organizing and using its leverage effectively, the masses will learn from it, follow it, develop their consciousness in and through it. Such a party can become the best means for breaking out of the trap of capitalist misery and harnessing the enormous revolutionary potential of the ghetto masses.

The nature of an independent black party

The Newark, Detroit and other uprisings that rocked the country during the summer of 1967 have raised some basic questions in the minds of many militants. They ask: Hasn't the black liberation movement already gone beyond the stage of electoral politics? Isn't it too late to be talking about assembling the forces to build a party, about independent campaigns, candidates and programs? Aren't we close to the final showdown with the white capitalist power structure? Hasn't the time of the bullet superseded the casting of the ballot? Isn't resort to armed struggle in the form of guerrilla warfare the only effective mode of action on the agenda? Don't we need an army, or at least dedicated bands of guerrilla fighters, rather than a political party?

Such questions are not out of place; they have been imperatively posed by the fierce conflicts which have occurred in many cities and will flare up again. They have to be squarely faced and answered by all those concerned with the progress and prospects of the liberation struggle. Here is our view.

The explosions of 1967 testify to the revolutionary temper and potential of the black freedom struggle and mark its highest point. They demonstrate that the Afro-American minority is destined to play a vanguard role in the social changes leading up to the American revolution. Although the uprisings ran out of steam in a few days or were put down with heavy casualties and suffering, they are an inspiration to all genuine revolutionists, black or white.

With few exceptions the inhabitants of the ghetto did not feel that they met with defeat. On the contrary, their self-confidence and combativeness have been enhanced. By shattering the image of their alleged docility, they taught an important lesson to the ruling class. They also dealt a stiff blow to the myth that mass action by workers is no longer effective in modern, sophisticated, urbanized America. Finally they showed that the demand for black control of the black community is not a fringe notion in the ghettos but expresses the will of its residents.

While these determined demonstrations go far to refute the concept that the ghetto is "powerless," it would be unwise to overlook or keep quiet about the shortcomings of these historic actions. The uprisings were spontaneous—nobody planned or instigated them, despite the lies of the witch-hunters who are looking for scapegoats and excuses for devising new repressive measures. They were uncontrolled eruptions against unbearable conditions.

Although in size and scope they were the most impressive upheavals the United States has ever seen, they did not go beyond the stage of protest. After they had subsided, the relation of forces had changed but the lives of the ghetto dwellers were not any better. For example, the social and economic conditions in Watts remain essentially the same two years after the explosion there. The black freedom fighters still face the task of organizing the forces required to abolish the root causes of their degradation.

Malcolm X stated that the revolutionary movement must resolve to achieve "freedom by any means necessary." The specific question at hand now is: What means are now necessary to best advance the struggle at this point? That is, what tactics are in order under the given conditions?

Some advanced elements in the black communities insist that only armed struggle is warranted and any one who advises different tactics is cowardly or worse. They believe that any sort of political organization and action is incompatible with direct action. Their militancy is undeniable. But small bands of men, however courageous and self-sacrificing, cannot serve as a substitute for the organized urban masses.

The main task at the present rudimentary stage of the struggle for power is not to hurl unorganized, unprepared masses against the most highly organized, centralized and formidable power in the entire world, and even less to pit small and scattered groups of armed men against it. The basic problem is how most effectively to organize and educate these masses and equip them with the proper understanding, leadership, program and perspectives.

The time for armed struggle does not come merely because a few daring rebels are ready for it, talk about it or want it. It ripens as the culmination of a prolonged process of mass mobilization after other available methods of action have been tried and found wanting.

So far as the black masses are concerned, the stage of electoral activity has not been exhausted; in fact, it has hardly been tried. The same black people who came out into the streets and tore up districts in Newark, Detroit and elsewhere have still not broken with the Democratic Party, the party of the white supremacists, exploiters and war-makers!

A year after the big uprising in Cleveland and only a few months after Newark and Detroit, almost 95 per cent of Cleveland's registered Afro-Americans turned out to nominate and elect the black man Stokes as mayor on the Democratic ticket. In some ghetto districts Stokes received every black vote. In the same way a black mayor was elected in the steel center of Gary, Indiana.

Some will say that these developments only go to show how backward black people are. What's actually bad is not their use of electoral action to get rid of hated city officials but the fact that this weapon was used along the old lines and is still wielded by the same old hands. The black voters in Cleveland, Gary and other places will now have to go through more experiences of disillusionment with their black Democratic mayors. Black militants can hasten this process only by showing an alternative acceptable to the masses at their present level of consciousness—and nothing will meet this need better today than advocacy of a political party controlled by the masses and not their oppressors.

The ultra-left opponents of political action, or abstainers from it, are mistaken in four respects. 1. They hastily and uncritically transfer tactics and techniques which proved applicable at the advanced stage of the Chinese, Cuban and Vietnam revolutions to the far different, more complex and less matured conditions in the United States. 2. They one-sidedly believe that electoral action is incompatible with any form of direct action whereas the two can be combined or alternated to the advantage of both. 3. They proceed on the assumption that electoral action has been bypassed or outmoded when it is only entering a new phase. 4. Finally, in their exclusive preoccupation with armed struggle and associated forms of direct action, however legitimate these may be, they fail to come to grips with the most pressing problem of the present hour. That is the barely begun task of unifying into a cohesive force and educating the millions of ghetto dwellers who must shoulder the colossal assignment of overturning white supremacy and radically transforming capitalist

America. This prolonged and difficult job cannot be impatiently waved aside or skipped over by those who aspire to lead the black revolution.

That first requires the organization of these masses into a formidable and independent political force. Blowing up the Democratic Party would be an explosion of greater magnitude and consequences than tearing down a hundred stores. Smashing the two-party system—which the strategically situated black minority can accomplish—would do a thousand times more damage to the structure of American capitalism than burning down a whole city. These political objectives can be achieved with a powerful and well-organized independent black party.

What makes an independent black political party possible

What makes it both possible and urgent for black people to build an independent party, which the ruling class does not want, is the system of racial segregation which the ruling class created and intends to maintain.

Segregation and urbanization have brought the black people together *physically*, especially in the politically decisive big cities where in many cases they will soon be a majority of the inhabitants. Segregation and discrimination are also bringing the black masses together *psychologically*. It is now necessary to unite them *politically* on local, state and national levels.

The rulers of this country do not care to have black people think of themselves as a distinctive group—with group consciousness, group interests and group objectives. They go to considerable trouble to persuade blacks to accept the same myths about "individual progress" that they have used to brainwash white Americans. But in pursuing their own ends the dominant powers create the very thing they don't want. They not only force black people to live together; they also make them feel, think and react together and in similar ways to their oppression. The ghetto whose original function was to facilitate economic exploitation and to split the working class now plays an additional role unwelcome to the powers that be. It can serve as a base and force to unite black people politically.

If the capitalist class had abolished racism, an independent black party would not have been possible. If the labor movement had broken with capitalist politics and launched a revolutionary struggle along socialist lines that included the abolition of racism as one of its key demands, an independent black party would not have been likely. Such a party is now possible and likely because capitalist development has created the objective preconditions for it and closed off other avenues for effective political struggle, and because other anticapitalist forces, at least for the time being, have not opened up alternative roads for political opposition.

A base for an independent black party already exists and only awaits serious efforts to organize it. In mid-1966, according to a national poll made in *Newsweek*, 7 percent of the black people said they were in favor of operating as a "separate force" in politics, rather than through the Democrats or Republicans. That survey was made prior to the ouster of Adam Clayton Powell from Congress, which added greatly to resentment against the two major parties and disillusionment in working through them.

To be sure, 7 per cent is a small minority of the black population. But it is not an insignificant minority when an independent party has not yet been started or widely discussed, when it is only an idea, and before it has had any opportunity to show it can be established, work and produce favorable results. No political party *starts* with a majority of the people it hopes to enlist. The majority has to be won over, through struggle and education, by the more far-seeing minority that creates the party. Seven per cent of the black population amounts to a million or so adults and young people in their late teens. This is surely enough to launch a new party and sustain it long enough to carry out the tasks of educating, mobilizing and winning the adherence of a majority of Afro-Americans.

An independent black party can unite the Afro-American masses of this country, North and South, urban and rural. It can draw into activity millions who have felt that politics is futile and it can raise the political understanding of black people as a whole. It can take over the political life of the black community. In fact, this is the only way the slogan and concept of black power can be politically realized.

In all areas where black people are a majority, it can run and elect to office representatives who will not have obligations and allegiances to the capitalist parties and who will be responsible to the black community. A well-organized continuing black party, democratically controlled by its ranks, can control its own candidates in office more strictly and thoroughly than any committee that is set up for a single election campaign can do.

A strong black party will not only isolate and destroy the Democratic and Republican party machinery in the ghetto, doing away with two-timing political Uncle Toms, but will bring about a vast increase in black representation at all levels of government. Instead of five or six members of Congress who are tied to the capitalist parties and subject to their pressures, there could be 50 or 60 who owed their election and allegiance to an independent black party. Instead of a relatively few state legislators and municipal councilmen, there could be a large bloc of hundreds and thousands of black men and women elected to office as genuine representatives and spokesmen for their people. They could take over the operation of big cities in the North as well as small counties in the South. For the first time black Americans would have a political voice that really spoke for them, a political weight that could not be ignored or swept aside, a political power that could make itself felt, both for defensive and offensive purposes.

Representatives of the black people will be able to govern in areas where they are a majority. In other areas, including Congress, they will be able to fight and or negotiate more effectively than in the past. Both in situations that call for political combat and situations that call for political negotiating, the representatives of an independent black party would compel respect from both their foes and their friends and would extract far more concessions than Negro Democrats and Republicans ever have done up to now because they would be bargaining from a position of strength.

If an independent black party accomplished only these things, its organization would be justified. But by its mere existence it will accomplish other things as well. The massive withdrawal of black voters from the Democratic Party—not to the Republicans, not into electoral abstention, but into a powerful party of their own—would shake the political structure of this country from top to bottom.

This comes from one of the basic facts of American life today. The black man can't stand up erect, can't even exercise his democratic rights (that's what independent political organization would signify), without repercussions spreading throughout the United States. White men, rich or poor, upper or middle or lower class, would have to move over or stand up to or alter their stance in some other ways. When large numbers of black people act on their own, a lot of other people, like it or not, will have to act and react too. When black people will move on their own account in the political field, others will also find themselves moving politically, or being moved.

The Democratic Party is usually predominant not because it is controlled by the capitalists (this fact is kept hidden or denied as much as possible). Its strength comes from the support received from a combination of sizeable non-capitalist forces—the unions, segments of the middle class, the unemployed, the pensioners and retirees along with the great majority of black people. The defection of the black voters will create an immediate crisis for this Democratic coalition. Without the black vote, the Democrats will be unable to carry the big cities and thereby have great difficulties in winning national elections and control of the White House or Congress. Since the Democratic coalition is bound together not by any principles or identity of interests, but by the belief that it can win national and lesser elections, its growing incapacity to do so will undermine the coalition's reasons for existence and in the end break it up.

Inside the unions those elements that are discontented with the pro-Democratic policy of the bureaucracy (and they are more numerous than is now apparent) will be strengthened and find it easier to win support for a struggle to establish an independent labor party. Old alignments will disintegrate and new ones will be formed. An independent party will be the best means for black people to protect and promote their welfare. It will also be the best way for them to forge new alliances with other non-capitalist forces in the conditions that will ensue after the two-party system crumbles.

Back in Reconstruction days after the Civil War,

political action by black freedmen in the South improved educational facilities, equalized taxes, cut down illiteracy, abolished imprisonment for debt and instituted many other reforms in city, county and state governments. Picture what unified political action by millions of Afro-Americans could accomplish today!

The nature of an independent black party

The character of an independent black party will, of course, be determined by its founders and members in accord with the needs and possibilities as they will see them at the time the party is organized. Without being able at this time to answer such questions concretely, it is nevertheless possible on the basis of past experience to discern certain problems that the builders of an independent black party will have to be concerned about both in the preparatory and initial phases of its organization.

How radical will such a party be? In terms of the political spectrum in the United States, a political party created to the left of the Democratic Party and in opposition to it will inescapably be labeled radical. How radical it will actually be, and what kind of radicalism it will actually express, will depend on the composition and outlook of the leaders and forces who launch the party and their evolution as they operate in the political arena. If, to them, independence of the capitalist parties means independence from capitalist politics, then it will surely be a radical party. The chances of this are strong because black militants and revolutionaries will probably be the chief advocates and founders of an independent party. But in the final analysis the degree of its radicalism will depend on the relationship of forces inside the groups that form and compose the new party.

Will it be a purely electoral party, or a party seeking to intervene and involve the masses in every area of struggle—economic and social as well as political—that affects the interests of black people? Will it seek to only elect candidates to office or will it also seek to mobilize and educate the masses by participating in and leading rent strikes, boycotts, demonstrations for jobs and control of decent schools, against police brutality and military interventions against colonial freedom fighters like the war in Vietnam? It is hard to see how an independent black party could become a mass force without following the practice of total involvement.

Will it be an all-black party (like the Freedom Now Party of 1963–4) or a party controlled and led by blacks (like the Lowndes County Freedom Party)? This is a question of tactical expediency, not of principle. Both approaches have advantages and drawbacks which will have to be carefully weighed.

The founders of the Freedom Now Party believed that an all-black organization would be more attractive to the black masses. Some of them still thought this was the best approach after the Freedom Now Party collapsed, while others felt it had been a mistake, not because of what white people thought about it but because they concluded it had been a deterrent to the recruitment of black supporters.

The founders of the Lowndes County Freedom Party in Alabama, on the other hand, left membership open to anyone who accepted its program and worked loyally for it. Despite this, control and leadership of the party remain with black people. The feeling among young militants in the North today is decidedly in favor of all-black organizations and they are likely to demand an all-black party when one is formed.

Just as it is difficult to envisage an independent black party confining itself exclusively to electoral activity, so it is difficult to imagine that its program would be restricted to so-called "racial" issues alone. Of course an independent black party will proceed from the needs of the black community but this very concern will inevitably lead it to consider positions and take actions on the most vital and urgent national and international issues.

When it opposes the drafting of black youth to kill colored people in Vietnam, it will be impelled to take a position for or against the war itself; its representatives in Congress will have to vote for or against military appropriations. When it demands jobs for blacks, it will have to take a stand on the fight for a shorter work week, a minimum wage, adequate compensation for all the unemployed. When it demands funds to replace the slums with decent housing for black people, it will have to take a position on the national budget and how it is divided. When it demands the right to control the schools in the black community, it will also have to take a position on the source of taxes and the way they are allocated.

Inevitably too, at some point, an independent black party will have to decide whether decent conditions of life, equality and freedom for the black people are really attainable under capitalism or whether a basically different, non-exploitative system is necessary—and whether a change of such magnitude can be effected through reform or requires revolutionary mass struggle. This will squarely pose the issue of capitalism versus socialism to the leaders, members and supporters of a party of black emancipation.

In the early stages many important and fundamental questions of program and perspective will very likely be left untouched, or even misjudged, as tends to happen at the beginning of every new party. These will have to be thought through and fought out in the course of the party's development as it grapples with the problems involved in creating a better life for all Afro-Americans.

Two pioneer experiences and their lessons

The two most significant recent experiments in independent black political organization have been the defunct Freedom Now Party and the apparently thriving Lowndes County Freedom Party of Alabama. What lessons do they teach?

Some opponents of independent black political action or downhearted former supporters of it contend that the attempt to build the Freedom Now Party turned out to be such a sad failure that all future efforts along that line are bound to be unsuccessful. From this negative judgment they conclude that the only realistic course now is to try and take over the Democratic Party in the ghetto and use it for the black community's purposes. They disregard the fact that this policy has been tried much longer and has given far poorer results.

Others propose some version of a "third force" that will be a pressure group but not a political party. Still others look for a third party like the Wallace Progressive Party of 1948 or talk about a "peace party" ticket.

In dismissing any future forms of independent black politics, they forget that all new and enduring political formations in American history or elsewhere have had short-lived predecessors. The Republican Party, launched in 1854, was preceded by the Liberty and Free Soil parties of the 1840s. John Brown's band failed to overturn the slave power or abolish chattel slavery—but it prepared the way for the Civil War that did. Jet travel is common today. Yet the first attempts to build airplanes either crashed or never got off the ground.

The truth is that the project of an independent black party did not get a fair and full trial from the founders of the Freedom Now Party and any subsequent attempt will have to understand the mistakes that were made to avoid repeating them.

The organization of the Freedom Now Party was not undertaken in a sufficiently serious, systematic and sustained way. A new mass party cannot simply be proclaimed; it has to be created by passing through a series of stages. The skeleton and backbone of the coming party has to be constituted through an initial stage of education and propaganda devoted to developing and clarifying its basic ideas, testing out its program, and training its cadres. Only when this indispensable preliminary groundwork is completed can the founding forces reach out and win over large numbers.

The national founders of the Freedom Now Party mixed up these two main stages and tried to do everything all at once. They thought it possible to leap over the tough preliminary chores of gathering, consolidating and educating the initial core. Then when the required organizers, administrators, educators, writers and all the rest did not come around rather quickly in substantial numbers, they became discouraged and gave up.

In the state of Michigan the Freedom Now Party did enlist a few hundred activists and manage to get on the ballot and run an election campaign in 1964. But there too the leadership attempted to rush through or skip over inescapable stages. Instead of concentrating at the start in clarifying the nature and problems of the new party for themselves and their followers and instead of developing a realistic long-range as well as an immediate objective, they pinned all their hopes on securing a big vote and possibly electing a few candidates. They counted on so impressive a showing on the first try that it would bring large numbers into the party right away.

Most of the Michigan leaders became discouraged when the party received only five thousand votes. Instead of regarding this support for a new, untried, unpopularized, largely unexplained movement as the beginning basis for sustained education and organization, they saw the low vote as evidence of total failure.

If in place of exorbitant expectations, they had been guided by a more realistic approach, the party might have survived, grown and spread to other places. The quick collapse of the Freedom Now Party did not prove that the black masses would not support and join an independent party. It only showed that they won't go for it in a rush and all together at the first call. They will have to be convinced and won over, not by a one-shot crack at the ballot box, but by persevering education and organization.

The main point to be learned from the Freedom Now Party experience is that the founders of a new party will first have to organize themselves properly before they will be able to organize large numbers successfully.

Like the Freedom Now Party, the Lowndes County Freedom Party clearly opposes both the Democratic and Republican parties and seeks to create an alternative to them. But it is being built on a more realistic basis. It was not proclaimed as a full-fledged political party as soon as the idea struck a few pioneers. Instead, it was discussed at great length by its founders, soberly, in detail, and with careful attention to local needs, possibilities and peculiarities. This preliminary stage of discussion, when the movement was known as the Lowndes County Freedom Organization, unified and educated the founders and gave them a perspective, trusted leaders and the elements of an agreed-upon structure for going forward to the launching of the Freedom Party itself.

Some members and sympathizers of the Lowndes County Freedom Party expected it to win the very first election it contested in November 1966 because black people are a majority in the county. They underestimated the intimidation and pressure applied by the Democrats and the difficulties of conducting an election campaign for the first time. The new Freedom Party did not win; its highest vote was 42 per cent. But its leaders and most of its members were not crushed by the outcome. Armed with a long-range outlook, they took the result in their stride and have set about to do better on the next try.

Thanks to its foresighted and careful planning, the Lowndes County Freedom Party has a well-defined organizational structure which facilitates active participation by its members and democratic decision making. Its candidates and leaders are expected to respect these decisions. Through constant education and propaganda it has sought to unify the black community and has displayed considerable skill and flexibility in bringing along most sections of the black community without sacrificing any of its basic principles or purposes.

While bidding for power and office through the ballot, it functions the year around to improve the living conditions of the black population through such projects as building a library, providing milk for children, etc. It has taken measures to ensure the self-defense of its supporters against racist terror attacks. It tries to better the conditions of the black people in all respects.

It remains to be seen whether it will continue to grow and become so deep-rooted that it cannot be disoriented or destroyed. In any event, it sets an example and provides a model for other black communities, North and South. If an independent black political movement can survive and grow under such difficult and isolated circumstances, how much easier could this job be done in a Harlem or a Watts!

The problem of allies and alliances

It is in the very nature and logic of political struggle to seek allies. Even majorities seek and make alliances. The question is not whether an independent black party would seek alliances but what kind and with whom.

The necessity of alliances is not altered by the fact that Afro-Americans are part of a nonwhite majority in the world and even less by the existence of differences with prospective allies. Alliances are made specifically with forces and movements with whom an organization is not in essential or complete agreement. If there was complete agreement between the two, unity rather than alliance would be on the agenda. Practical agreements are made with forces which disagree on some or many matters. Alliances are concluded on actions and aims on which there is a coincidence of interests, even if only for a temporary period, while "agreeing to disagree" on other things.

This right to disagree on some points while working together on others is crucial. Without this right there is not an alliance of equals but a dependent relationship of a subordinate to a superior power. The existence of an independent black party would safeguard Afro-Americans against the wrong kinds of alliance. They would not be forced into unfavorable or unequal tieups because an independent organization always has the option of getting up and walking out. It is not necessary to agree to any move, tactic or strategy which will injure your cause so long as you are independent and able to withdraw and act on your own.

At this juncture the major alliances possible for an independent black party would be international. The American ruling class that oppresses and exploits black people at home has a large and growing list of enemies abroad. It is feasible and imperative for Afro-Americans to forge ties with the victims of U.S. imperialism who are still in shackles, with those who have broken them, and with those who are in the process of breaking them. Malcolm X was stressing and striving to effect such alliances at the time of his assassination because he knew what healthy effects they could have on the progress of the liberation struggle within the United States. Stokely Carmichael's speech at the OLAS Conference in Havana and other Third World capitals demonstrate that such alliances are in the making.

Once an independent black party has the power and acquires the skill to seek and make alliances on its own terms, then it will also be possible to create useful alliances with domestic forces. Among these will be the rebel youth, especially among the students; the antiwar movement; the Spanish-speaking people (Puerto Ricans and Mexican-Americans); the American Indians whose plight has been neglected by almost all the forces in the country; poor white workers; and radical opponents of both capitalism and the trade union bureaucracies. While none of these elements may approach problems in exactly the way black militants do, those who are enemies of the enemies of black people at home can become partners on certain issues and for certain stretches of the road, whatever their staying power in the long run.

Cooperation with allies is part and parcel of the strategy of splitting white America and driving wedges into its constituent elements with conflicting interests so that some whites will fight others to the benefit of the black people. An independent black party would best enable Afro-Americans to employ this tactic without surrendering their own interests, unity, autonomy or freedom of action. Successful maneuvering along these lines would set an example for other potential anticapitalist forces by encouraging them to break with capitalist politics and showing them what independent political action can achieve.

Why the SWP supports independent black political action
The Socialist Workers Party believes that only a revolution taking economic and political power away from the capitalist exploiters and abolishing the system of production for profit can cleanse this country of racism and enable Americans to live in harmony, prosperity and equality with one another and with the rest of the world.

The Socialist Workers Party opposes the capitalist system and its political agents who run the Democratic and Republican Parties. It exposes all attempts to hoodwink and lure the working people, black or white, into supporting the candidates of these basically white supremacist and anti-labor parties on such pretexts as "it's the man, and not the party, that counts." The Socialist Workers Party does not endorse "people's fronts," anti-monopoly coalitions, "lesser evil" choices, "third forces," so-called "peace candidates" or any other formations which have not clearly and cleanly cut their ties with the capitalist parties and asserted their independence of capitalist politics.

On the other hand, the Socialist Workers Party will support and defend those political forces and movements which represent a genuine breakaway from capitalist politics, whether or not they are socialist-minded or oriented. Thus it advocates the creation of an independent labor party by trade unions and would back such a progressive step, whatever criticisms it might have of a labor party's program and leadership.

Similarly, the Socialist Workers Party favors the formation of an independent party uniting Afro-Americans in political struggle for their just rights and freedom. It believes that black people have the democratic right to decide their own destiny and that, without such a political instrument, they cannot effectively advance their immediate well-being or attain their ultimate goals. That is why the Socialist Workers Party supported the Freedom Now Party and supports the Lowndes County Freedom Party.

There is no contradiction between adhering to the ideas of revolutionary socialism and championing an all-black party. To be sure, the one is consciously opposed to the capitalist order whereas the other may be only partially and potentially directed against its domination. But both will stand arrayed against a common enemy in the capitalist ruling class and should travel along the same road toward the same destination.

Because black people are the most exploited, oppressed and aroused part of the population, it is reasonable to expect that they will become the first mass force to cut loose from the Democratic Party coalition and blaze a trail for others to follow. If they should establish an influential party of their own which carried through the fight against oppression and exploitation to the end, black Americans can be the vanguard of radical change in this country and play a decisive role in revolutionizing its political life.

SECTION VI. TWO CAMPAIGNS BY CARL STOKES

In the 1965 Cleveland mayoralty race, Carl Stokes, a Black candidate, lost the Democratic primary and ran in the general election independent of the Democratic and Republican candidates. The Socialist Workers Party supported Stokes in that race—criticizing his reformist program and affiliation to the Democratic Party while pointing out that his campaign was independent of the capitalist parties, using that fact to help promote the idea of independent Black political action. The article "Cleveland Negro Almost Upset Machine" by Eric Reinthaler describes this campaign.

In 1967, when Stokes won the Democratic party nomination and was elected mayor of Cleveland, the SWP strongly opposed this campaign. In the same year Richard Hatcher, also a Black Democrat, was elected mayor of Gary, Indiana. The meaning of these campaigns is discussed by Elizabeth Barnes in "Stokes' Cleveland Victory" and "Stokes-Hatcher Victory: A Real Gain for Blacks?" and by Eric Reinthaler in "Why President Johnson Favors Stokes for Cleveland Mayor." Stokes was mayor until 1971.

Cleveland Negro Almost Upset Machine
by Eric Reinthaler

CLEVELAND, O.—Carl B. Stokes, independent Negro candidate for mayor of Cleveland, received 85,375 votes in the recent election and was nosed-out in a photo-finish race by incumbent Democrat Ralph Locher who won with 87,833 votes, according to the unofficial count. Stokes has filed action with the Board of Elections to prevent Locher's certification until charges of irregularities are documented and a decision on a recount is made.

On election night over 1,000 Stokes supporters gathered at campaign headquarters, cheering as returns showed the independent candidate getting 90 percent of the vote in the Negro wards.

Papers Warn

Cleveland newspapers, well aware of the upset in the local political relationship of forces, are now cautioning Locher on his future course, pointing out that he must respond to the pressing needs of the Negro community.

Stokes, a Democratic state legislator, bypassed the Democratic primary and filed over 30,000 nominating signatures to run as an independent. He ran with the support of many leaders of the Negro community and with the support of such organizations as CORE, the Freedom Fighters, and ADA.

The Socialist Workers Party gave Stokes critical support based on the character of his campaign, which was independent of and opposed to the Democratic and Republican Parties. The SWP holds that the question of Negro representation in government is of vital concern not only to Negroes but to democratic-minded whites as well.

SWP criticism of the Stokes campaign was on his program, especially the question of a meaningful program for jobs, and Stokes' emphasis on "attract-

Reprinted from the *Militant*, November 22, 1965

ing industry back to Cleveland." Shortcomings on these issues conspired against a full mobilization of his voting potential. However, despite questions of program, the election decisively refutes the notion that a successful campaign can only be mounted within the Democratic Party.

While Stokes' program in and of itself could not solve the questions of jobs, housing and other problems facing the Negro people and poor whites in this community, his campaign points the way to the kind of independent political action necessary to force more basic solutions to those needs. The impact of the election has been a heightened solidarity and increased confidence of Cleveland Negroes. It has had a traumatic effect on the Democratic Party, the press and the AFL-CIO.

Slimmest Margin

Ralph Locher, the Democratic mayor, who was re-elected by the narrowest margin in the history of Cleveland mayoralty elections, had the support of Cleveland's two daily newspapers, most of the Negro Democratic city councilmen, and the Cleveland AFL-CIO.

In the last weeks of the campaign, the Cleveland AFL-CIO publicly endorsed him as the "safe" candidate and accused Stokes of injecting the "racial issue" into the campaign.

The Republican candidate was Ralph Perk, who polled 41,109 votes. The fourth candidate was Ralph McAllister, member of the Cleveland school board, and president of the school board during last year's school boycott. McAllister had the support of the most prejudiced and backward elements of the white community, and received 22,660 votes. The last weeks of the campaign saw inroads in McAllister support by Locher's backers who were successful in pointing out that unless McAllister supporters switched their votes to Locher, Stokes, a Negro, would be elected mayor.

Will Try Again

Stokes announced that he would run again for mayor two years from now. Meanwhile Locher asked Stokes and the other defeated candidates to join with him to "bring unity and harmony to the city." Stokes, however, analyzed the vote as rejection of "Locherism and all it stands for." He added, "It is fantastic that a man in office three years and backed by both newspapers, the Democratic Party and organized labor could not have polled more than 37 percent of the vote." Stokes charged the Democratic Party and the Cleveland AFL-CIO with whipping up racial animosities against him. He said, "The racial issue was never an issue, really, until the Democratic and labor leadership made it one."

Stokes' support in the Negro community was demonstrated in Ward 25 where the Negro Democratic councilman endorsed Locher. The vote in that ward was: Stokes, 8,555; Locher, 411; Perk, 263; McAllister, 24. Similar overwhelming majorities for Stokes in the ghetto wards do not reflect, however, more than 70 percent of the voting potential in the Negro community as a whole. Rather than indicating apathy alone, the number not voting reflects inadequate independent organization and a certain lack of confidence in the Negro Democratic politicians who have been elected to office in Cleveland over the past years.

In the campaign Stokes opposed the enactment of a city income tax and opposed increases in home owners' taxes. He proposed a city "value added in manufacture tax." The tax would be on the value manufacturers here add to the products they make from raw materials. For example, if a company took $3.00 worth of raw materials and manufactured a $5.00 product, the tax would be on the $2.00 in added value. This tax, Stokes said, would bring $12 million annual revenue into the city treasury.

Muny Light

At the same time, Stokes advocated sale of the city's Municipal light plant because of its "inefficiency." The Muny Light Plant, however, affords lower electric rates to thousands of Clevelanders and serves as a brake on the rate schedules of the privately owned Cleveland Electric Illuminating Company. Some Stokes supporters, including the SWP, felt that he should have called for the expansion of the Muny Light Plant and its services.

The Freedom Fighters, a number of individuals, and the SWP regarded a position for a 30 hour week at 40 hours pay for all city employes as a concrete proposal to create several thousand new jobs in Cleveland. If Stokes had adopted this plank he could have attracted wider ghetto support and evoked a more favorable response from labor's rank and file.

Review Board

CORE, Freedom Fighters, the United Freedom Movement, a number of churches and fraternal groups had also supported the proposal for a citizens police review board. Stokes did not put this into his program arguing that the conduct of the police department is ultimately the responsibility of the mayor's office and that if he were elected his office would always be open to hear complaints which he promised he would act on.

The strength shown by Stokes may force the union movement to question the policy of tying itself to the Democratic Party and to seriously consider the factor of a growing independent constituency in the Negro community which may well be the decisive factor in future elections in major industrial cities like Cleveland.

The action of Cleveland Federation of Labor head Patrick J. O'Malley in doing the racist dirty work for the Democratic Party in this campaign has evoked bitter resentment among Negro unionists. Other local labor leaders are sharply critical of O'Malley's role in the elections and repercussions are expected. The fact that neither President Johnson nor any important administration spokesman intervened in Locher's behalf showed the concern of the Democratic Party nationally with the danger of losing the Negro vote.

Why President Johnson Favors Stokes for Cleveland Mayor
by Eric Reinthaler

CLEVELAND—Carl B. Stokes, Negro Democrat who won the nomination for mayor of Cleveland in the Oct. 3 primary, is clearly the preferred candidate of the ruling class. Stokes has the endorsement of the Cuyahoga County Democratic organization. Both Cleveland daily papers endorsed Stokes in the primary, and the *Plain Dealer* just endorsed him over Republican candidate Seth Taft.

In 1965 Stokes ran as an independent for mayor and narrowly missed election. A short time later, Vice President Humphrey came to Cleveland to hold a private meeting with Stokes. Last year Stokes was reelected as a Democrat to the State Legislature.

Vietnam

Stokes' campaign budget was said to be $160,000. When questioned on the war in Vietnam, he stated, "I stand with my President." This was true in spite of the fact that a large number of the more than 10,000 signers of the petition for an antiwar referendum in Cleveland were from the black community.

Stokes supported Republican Governor Rhodes' Ohio Bond Commission proposal, which was a give-away program to large corporate interests. Stokes favored selling the Cleveland Municipal Light Plant, the publicly owned low-rate company, to the privately owned Cleveland Electric Illuminating Co. Several key figures in the latter, like Ralph Besse and Cyrus Eaton, were avid backers and financers of the Stokes campaign.

In the *Cleveland Press*, Oct. 7, political editor Richard L. Maher wrote:

> Months ago it was disclosed here that President Johnson wants desperately to elect a Negro mayor in Cleveland, and that Stokes was his choice.
>
> Political observers feel that Johnson has written off Ohio, which he carried by a million votes in 1964, that he wants to get Stokes elected to use this as a campaign argument in other northern areas to hold large blocs of Negroes in line in 1968.

Reprinted from the *Militant*, November 6, 1967

In the election two years ago, Stokes was opposed by the Democratic incumbent, the Republican candidate and by a rabid white supremacist. That election was a massive expression of the possibility of mounting a successful campaign outside the Democratic and Republican parties. The extension of it would have provided a powerful impetus to black independent political action in other large cities.

The ruling class hopes to head off such a development. They believe that the expected Stokes victory in Cleveland will have a national impact, fostering illusions about the possibility of achieving a degree of "black power" within the framework of the Democratic Party.

The only problem is that the capitalist system, and the Democrats and Republicans who support it, cannot change the oppressive ghetto conditions which gave rise to the struggle for black power. Negro representation in the Democratic machine will not change this. It will only give the ruling parties a longer stranglehold on the ghettos

Stokes' Cleveland Victory
by Elizabeth Barnes

For the first time a black man has been nominated on the Democratic Party ticket for mayor of one of the nation's major cities. It happened in Cleveland on Oct. 3 when Carl Stokes defeated the present white mayor in the Democratic primary by a vote of 103,637 to 91,369.

This election reflected, in a negative way, the tremendous potential political power of black people. Seventy-four percent of Cleveland's black voters turned out and 95 percent of those pulled the lever for Stokes. In order to win Stokes had to split off only a small percentage of the white vote, since black people comprise a large section of the voters.

The Stokes victory is only one example of the effect that radicalization in the black community is having on the Democratic Party. In Gary, Ind., a town that is 58 percent black, the Democratic Party is also running an Afro-American mayoral candidate against a white Republican.

In Washington, D.C., where over half the population is black, President Johnson has appointed an Afro-American as the city's new commissioner and he has named five Afro-Americans to the nine-member District of Columbia City Council.

Democratic politicians are finding that they must at least appear to be responding to the needs of the black community if they are to maintain the support of Afro-American voters. The Democratic Party is dependent on the black vote in order to win, both in the cities and on a national level, and party leaders hope that by making a few superficial changes they can keep black people pulling the lever for their candidates. They are thus looking for more black candidates to run as Democratic Party window dressing.

After the Stokes election, for example, an article in the *New York Times* commented that Democratic politicians hoped Stokes would be the Democratic Party "equivalent" of the Republican's Senator Brooke.

Ironically, it was Stokes himself who helped alert the Democratic Party to the danger of black voters leaving the party fold when in 1965 he ran as an independent candidate for mayor and was only barely defeated by incumbent Mayor Locher in a photo-finish vote of 85,375 to 87,833.

Although both Stokes and Hatcher (the Democratic candidate for mayor of Gary) have had to fight county Democratic Party chairmen in their areas, they have received enthusiastic support from more sophisticated party leaders and supporters, who realize they need a few black faces to help cover up their real role as guardians of this racist system. Vice President Humphrey immediately responded to the Stokes victory by stating that Carl Stokes "has

---

Reprinted from the *Militant*, October 16, 1967

the leadership qualities every great city needs."

Democratic Party supporters have pushed the lie that Stokes' election is proof that freedom can be won by working through the existing political setup. Bayard Rustin said it indicated that American society is capable of "accepting Negroes" and Stokes himself stated that the victory "vindicates my faith in American Democracy."

Stokes' political program is fully in accord with that of the Democratic Party. For example, his response to the black rebellion in Cleveland last year was to criticize the mayor for not calling in the National Guard fast enough. In addition he has successfully sponsored legislation enabling the state governor to send troops into the black community in Cleveland without getting the O.K. of the mayor.

Stokes may feel that "American democracy" has fulfilled his personal dreams, but in his position as window dressing for the Democratic Party he will only help to sow false illusions among the masses of black people about the nature of this party which is controlled lock, stock and barrel by the enemies of black people.

As SNCC members in Washington, D.C., pointed out after the appointment of the Afro-American as commissioner, it is not the fact that a candidate is black that determines whether he will be relevant to the needs of the black community. If Stokes is elected as mayor of Cleveland he will be able to do no more to solve the problems of black people than have the black Democratic Party politicians that black people have sent to Congress year after year.

Stokes-Hatcher Victory: A Real Gain for Blacks?
by Elizabeth Barnes

The electoral victories of Carl Stokes in Cleveland and Richard Hatcher in Gary have important implications for the future of the black liberation movement, but they will not change the conditions of black people in these cities. H. Rap Brown recently summed up the meaning of the Stokes election when he characterized it as "neo-colonialism" and called Stokes a "puppet of the Democratic Party and the U.S. government."

Both candidates received the support of the national Democratic Party. Such top Democrats as Humphrey and Kennedy made special efforts to aid their campaigns. And although Hatcher adapted more to the sentiments of the black community than did Stokes, both are in essential agreement with the ruling class on all important issues.

At the same time, the Stokes and Hatcher victories are important as a reflection of the heightened political and nationalist consciousness in the black community. Stokes and Hatcher were both elected because Afro-Americans in these two cities voted black. Hatcher received 95 percent of the black vote, and Stokes received 94.5 percent. In five black districts in Cleveland, Stokes' white opponent, Seth Taft, didn't get a *single vote*.

Although they are adapting to it by running black candidates, Democratic Party politicians do not like the nationalist or "race" consciousness that was reflected in the vote. Stokes faithfully kowtowed to their feelings by using the campaign slogan, "Don't vote for a Negro . . . Vote for a man."

Capitalist politicians are afraid that black people will start to feel the very real potential political power which they have if they unite to support, not a Democratic Party candidate, but a party of their own.

A Nov. 12 *New York Times* editorial summed up the feelings of many politicians when it commented, "Last Tuesday's elections in Cleveland, Gary and parts of the South translated 'black power,' that mischievous and opaque slogan, into the only meaningful terms it can have: political success achieved through the democratic process."

Reprinted from the *Militant*, November 20, 1967

Not only do those who run this country hope that the election of black candidates will dampen the struggle in the streets, but they hope it will keep black people loyal to the Democratic Party. Rowland Evans and Robert Novak, columnists for the *New York Post*, described the elections as constituting "a plus for the White House by averting a mass 1968 defection of Negro voters."

The results of the election give important clues as to what strategy is correct for the black struggle. First of all, they show definitively that the masses of black people are still looking to the electoral process and the Democratic Party to change things. The voters came out in record numbers. It was the biggest election turnout in the history of Gary, and the total Cleveland vote exceeded every year since 1933. In both cities, the percentage of registered Afro-Americans who voted was bigger than that of whites.

When black people voted for Stokes and Hatcher, they voted for men who have already shown clearly that they do not represent the black community on important issues. In a city where 10,000 signers of a recent petition for an antiwar referendum came from the black community, Stokes takes the position of "standing with the President" on Vietnam.

Both candidates have taken a tough attitude toward the black rebellions of this summer, and they can be expected to act not much differently from their white predecessors when new revolts occur. Stokes is opposed to a civilian police review board and has sponsored a bill in the state legislature regulating the sale of firearms.

It is a mistake to think that black people can be independent of the ruling class and remain within the Democratic Party, which the rulers control and finance. An editorial on the Hatcher-Stokes elections that appears in the Nov. 12 *Worker* shows no understanding of this fact. Hailing the "historic victories" of Stokes and Hatcher, the editorial draws the conclusion that "it is possible to challenge the present controllers of the country's political life in the Democratic and Republican parties and beat them on their home grounds by independent political action." Independent of whom? If Johnson, Humphrey, Kennedy and other such supporters of Hatcher and Stokes are not considered part of "the present controllers of the country's political life," then who is?

The lesson to be drawn from the election is the opposite of that reached by the *Worker*. It shows what potential power black people have if they enter politics outside of the Democratic Party. It shows it is the racist Democratic Party that needs the Afro-American voters, not vice versa.

The victory in Gary was especially illustrative of this, because Hatcher had the active opposition of the county Democratic machine. When Hatcher refused to become the complete tool of local Democratic Party Chairman John Krupa, the latter attacked Hatcher viciously and was reported to have made the statement that Hatcher was not the "right kind" of Negro. Krupa boasted that he would "groom" such a Negro candidate after Hatcher was defeated.

The desperation felt by the Democratic Party hacks in Gary was shown when they tried, literally, to steal the election by such crude methods as adding fictitious names to the election rolls and illegally crossing off names of black voters. When they were caught red-handed, a special three-judge panel forced Krupa, who also happens to be Secretary of the Election Board, to replace the names. As it turned out, the election was so close (39,330 to 37,941) that these votes probably made the difference.

A headline in the Oct. 29 Cleveland *Plain Dealer* reads, "Gary's Black Revolt Could Wreck Democrats." Although Hatcher's loyalty to the Democratic Party means that it is only the small potatoes Gary Democratic machine that could be "wrecked" as a result of this election—the headline reflects the constant fear aroused by the threat of black power. If black people had a political party which could provide a real alternative to the Stokes and Hatchers, it could challenge the Republicans and Democrats for control of many cities. It could split the white vote, even more than did the Stokes and Hatcher elections, if it were organized to fight for demands relevant to many whites—demands which are not being met by the two parties—such as an end to the war in Vietnam.

Stokes and Hatcher have already shown that they are going to disappoint those who voted for them. As a result there is an important opportunity for education on the need for independence from the Democratic Party and the ruling class and the need for an independent black political movement.

SECTION VII. THE BLACK PANTHER PARTY

In October 1966, Huey P. Newton and Bobby Seale organized the Black Panther Party for Self-Defense in Oakland, California. Both Newton and Seale were active in the struggles of the Black community and were inspired by many of the ideas of Malcolm X and the experiences of groups such as the Lowndes County Freedom Organization. This was reflected in the new organization's ten-point program.

Early in 1967, the organization became simply the Black Panther Party. In October of that year, Newton was framed up and imprisoned on the charge of murdering a policeman, and a broad, nationwide defense campaign for him was organized. By 1968, the party had begun to branch out to cities across the country, recruiting several thousand members and gaining widespread support for many of its ideas.

In that same year, the BPP also began to become involved in electoral politics. In Seattle, it launched a local campaign independent of the capitalist parties. However, the axis of the BPP's electoral efforts nationally centered on its alliance with the Peace and Freedom Party, an organization whose program was directed toward forming a third, "progressive," capitalist party. Eldridge Cleaver, the BPP's minister of information, became the PFP candidate for president.

Increasingly, the BPP began to move in an ultraleft direction, placing more and more emphasis on "picking up the gun," and retreating from involvement in the mass struggles of the Black community. Simultaneously, the U.S. government was carrying out one of the most brutal campaigns of repression ever unleashed on a political group in the U.S. Dozens of Panthers were murdered in cold-blooded political assassinations. Hundreds of others were framed up on various charges and thrown in jail. In addition, the FBI launched a massive disruption effort, utilizing informers, provocateurs, misinformation, and other types of undercover intrigues with the goal of paralyzing the party and intimidating its supporters.

This repression, combined with the Panthers' ultraleft errors, led to the decline of the organization. In 1971, a split occurred between the forces led by Newton and Seale and a group led by Cleaver. During this period, the BPP began to move in a rightward direction. It began to support Democratic party candidates, the ten-point program was discarded, and in 1973, Bobby Seale ran for mayor of Oakland, openly proclaiming himself to be a Democrat.

The first item printed in this section is the Panthers' ten-point program, drawn up in October 1966 and widely publicized by the party for the next several years. Following this are two articles describing the Panthers' involvement in the 1968 elections: one on the Seattle independent campaign and the other on the alliance with the Peace and Freedom Party. The article, "Retreat from a Strategy of Mass Action" by Derrick Morrison, is the second of a three-part series on the BPP that appeared in the *Militant*. "Why Did the Black Panther Party Split?" by Tony Thomas sums up some of the factors that led to the Panthers' decline; and the final article in the section describes the 1973 Seale campaign in Oakland.

The Black Panther Party Platform and Program

1. We want freedom. We want power to determine the destiny of our Black Community.

We believe that black people will not be free until we are able to determine our destiny.

2. We want full employment for our people.

We believe that the federal government is responsible and obligated to give every man employment or a guaranteed income. We believe that if the white American businessmen will not give full employment, then the means of production should be taken from the businessmen and placed in the community so that the people of the community can organize and employ all of its people and give a high standard of living.

3. We want an end to the robbery by the white man of our Black Community.

We believe that this racist government has robbed us and now we are demanding the overdue debt of forty acres and two mules. Forty acres and two mules was promised 100 years ago as restitution for slave labor and mass murder of black people. We will accept the payment in currency which will be distributed to our many communities. The Germans are now aiding the Jews in Israel for the genocide of the Jewish people. The Germans murdered six million Jews. The American racist has taken part in the slaughter of over fifty million black people; therefore, we feel that this is a modest demand that we make.

4. We want decent housing, fit for shelter of human beings.

We believe that if the white landlords will not give decent housing to our black community, then the housing and the land should be made into cooperatives so that our community with government aid can build and make decent housing for its people.

5. We want education for our people that exposes the true nature of this decadent American society. We want education that teaches us our true history and our role in the present-day society.

We believe in an educational system that will give to our people a knowledge of self. If a man does not have knowledge of himself and his position in society and the world, then he has little chance to relate to anything else.

6. We want all black men to be exempt from military service.

We believe that Black people should not be forced to fight in the military service to defend a racist government that does not protect us. We will not fight and kill other people of color in the world who, like black people, are being victimized by the white racist government of America. We will protect ourselves from the force and violence of the racist police and the racist military, by whatever means necessary.

7. We want an immediate end to POLICE BRUTALITY and MURDER of black people.

We believe we can end police brutality in our black community by organizing black self-defense groups that are dedicated to defending our black community from racist police oppression and brutality. The Second Amendment to the Constitution of the United States gives a right to bear arms. We therefore believe that all black people should arm themselves for self-defense.

8. We want freedom for all black men held in federal, state, county and city prisons and jails.

We believe that all black people should be released from the many jails and prisons because they have not received a fair and impartial trial.

9. We want all black people when brought to trial to be tried in court by a jury of their peer group or people from their black communities, as defined by the Constitution of the United States.

We believe that the courts should follow the United States Constitution so that black people will receive fair trials. The 14th Amendment of the U.S. Constitution gives a man a right to be tried by his peer group. A peer is a person from a similar economic, social, religious, geographical, environmental, historical and racial background. To do this the court will be forced to select a jury from the black community from which the black defendant came. We have been, and are being tried by all-white juries that have no understanding of the "average reasoning man" of the black community.

10. We want land, bread, housing, education, clothing, justice and peace. And as our major political objective, a United Nations-supervised plebiscite to be held throughout the black colony in which only black colonial subjects will be allowed to participate, for the purpose of determining the will of black people as to their national destiny.

When, in the course of human events, it becomes necessary for one people to dissolve the political bands which have connected them with another, and to assume, among the powers of the earth, the separate and equal station to which the laws of nature and nature's God entitle them, a decent respect to the opinions of mankind requires that they should declare the causes which impel them to the separation.

We hold these truths to be self-evident, that all men are created equal, that they are endowed by their Creator with certain unalienable rights; that among these are life, liberty, and the pursuit of happiness. That, to secure these rights, governments are instituted among men, deriving their just powers from the consent of the governed; that, whenever any form of government becomes destructive of these ends, it is the right of the people to alter or to abolish it, and to institute a new government, laying its foundation on such principles, and organizing its powers in such form, as to them shall seem most likely to effect their safety and happiness. Prudence, indeed, will dictate that governments long established should not be changed for light and transient causes; and, accordingly, all experience hath shown, that mankind are more disposed to suffer, while evils are sufferable, than to right themselves by abolishing the forms to which they are accustomed. But, when a long train of abuses and usurpations, pursuing invariably the same object, evinces a design to reduce them under absolute despotism, it is their right, it is their duty, to throw off such government, and to provide new guards for their future security.

Seattle Black Panther Party to Run Two Candidates for State Assembly
by Debbie Leonard and Will Reissner

SEATTLE—E.J. Brisker, minister of education of the Seattle Black Panther Party, told a crowd of nearly 100 at a Militant Labor Forum sponsored by the Young Socialist Alliance here July 5 that the Panthers will be running independent black candidates for the state legislature this fall.

On July 7 Black Panther captain Aaron Dixon officially announced the candidates at a rally of over 100 young Afro-Americans. The two candidates will be Brisker and Curtis Harris, Black Panther minister of defense, and they will run in the black community's 37th district, challenging two white Democratic incumbents and a black Democratic candidate supported by the 37th-district Democratic Committee.

Brisker is well-known in Seattle as a leader of the University of Washington Black Student Union and Seattle SNCC. Dixon, who announced the candidates at an outdoor rally, was recently sentenced to six months in jail along with two other defendants on charges stemming from a sit-in at Franklin High School. They are planning to appeal

Reprinted from the *Militant*, July 19, 1968

their convictions. (See July 5 *Militant*.)

E.J. Brisker, speaking at the rally, projected the independent Black Panther campaign as "the start of something very big—a history-making event." He pointed out that this was the first time the Black Panther Party was running a political campaign in its own name. The campaign will be based on the Black Panther Party's 10-point program which calls for "freedom and power to control the destiny of the black community" and demands full employment, decent housing, exemption from the draft and decent education for Afro-Americans.

The program further demands an end to the robbery of the black community by white businessmen, an end to police brutality, the release of all black prisoners and trial of Afro-Americans by their peers—Afro-Americans of similar age and economic status.

Locally, the Black Panther Party is calling for a civilian police review board, composed of members chosen by the community, with the power to subpoena, obtain police records, and indict cops for brutality. They are also demanding that several Afro-American "public defenders" be on call whenever needed to counsel arrested black citizens.

Brisker stressed that the focal point of the program is "black control of the black community"—control of housing, radio, newspapers, cops, schools, businesses, places of entertainment. "There should be a Malcolm X movie theatre, a Malcolm X coffee house and Martin Luther King and Malcolm X scholarship funds," he stated.

When questioned about the Black Panther Party's position on the draft, Brisker said, "We must take a hard position on the war in Vietnam. We have no business in Vietnam. The community must be prepared to defend black brothers against the military police when they try to rip a brother off." The Black Panther Party is proposing service within the black community as an alternative to the draft for Afro-Americans.

Curtis Harris declared that a major objective of his campaign would be increased communication between black people and making the Black Panther Party and its 10-point program known in the community. He urged supporters to get the word out about the campaign and reminded the audience, "The Black Panther Party has 200 representatives—not just two."

Besides this major political step of running independent black candidates, the Black Panther Party is engaged in a number of arenas of activity. They have organized patrols of the black community to keep an eye on the cops.

On a recent Saturday they organized a picket line of about 100 black residents in front of an Albertson's supermarket in the black community. They called for a boycott of Albertson's, one of the largest food chains in the Seattle area. They were protesting the firing of several black employees and the presence of armed Burns detectives—who are not found in stores in the white community. The picket line brought business to a standstill, and a special detachment of cops arrived on the scene. The pickets shouted at a black cop placed in front of the store, "Your brain has been washed inside and out by the honkies downtown."

Legal defense is another increasingly important aspect of Black Panther work. In addition to the sit-in convictions, five brothers have been charged with arson and disturbing the peace; they were arrested during the rebellion following Martin Luther King's assassination.

At the Militant Labor Forum Brisker stated, "America is an imperialist and colonial power." Afro-Americans are "an internally colonized people."

"American capitalism has the ability to absorb and nullify movements for change," Brisker said. As examples of this nullification, Brisker pointed to the role of black Democratic mayors like Walter Washington and Richard Hatcher, who, he said, are puppets of the white power structure.

At the Forum a collection of nearly $75 was raised for the Black Panther Party and for the defense of Seattle blacks framed up by the city administration. But the Panthers need much more money for their campaign work and for legal defense. Donations should be sent to their headquarters at 1127-½ 34th Ave., Seattle, Washington.

The Panther–Peace and Freedom Alliance
by Derrick Morrison

The alliance that the Black Panther Party has established with the Peace and Freedom Party poses a number of questions and problems for the black liberation movement. What is the nature of this alliance? Does it help or hinder the growth of the Black Panther Party as a vanguard formation?

Key to this question is how it relates to the building of a mass independent black party that can serve the people in the struggle for self-determination.

In the struggle for the liberation of the oppressed black nation, alliances and coalitions of varying types will be constructed along the way. Revolutionary black nationalist formations, such as SNCC, the Black Panther Party, and some black student organizations, seek to identify and align themselves with revolutionary movements and countries in Africa, Asia, and Latin America.

When Stokely Carmichael, formerly of SNCC, and two other SNCC members participated in the OLAS (Organization of Latin American Solidarity) conference last summer in Cuba, a symbolic alliance was created by OLAS with SNCC and other revolutionary elements in Afro-America. Cuba has since publicized and supported the activities of the Black Panther Party and the case of Huey P. Newton, minister of defense of the BPP. Just recently, the Black Panther Party has established close collaboration with the Brown Berets, a revolutionary Mexican-American group.

One of the central features of the alliances mentioned so far is that these coalitions involve revolutionary groups, or groups moving in a revolutionary direction. All of these alliances were formed to directly further and deepen the revolutionary struggle of Afro-America. They are political, or long-range alliances. The components of all of these alliances shared the common experience of being oppressed by and in opposition to the racist North American capitalist exploiters.

There are other types of alliances which develop around one or another particular issue. These

Reprinted from the *Militant*, September 20, 1968

specific or single-issue coalitions are formed on a short-term basis. These alliances may involve unity in staging a specific demonstration, such as a protest against the Vietnam war; or they may involve a committee to defend the victim of a frame-up or the rights of political groups that are attacked.

The Student Mobilization Committee is an example of a single-issue coalition. In this organization, people of varying political persuasions, from pacifism to revolutionary socialism, are united in an effort to end the war in Vietnam by bringing the troops home now. NBAWADU, the National Black Anti-War Anti-Draft Union, was a coalition of black organizations and people who wanted to organize the black community against the war and the draft. It was built mainly through the student strike of last April 26.

Last December, antiwar alliances were built to stage a week of demonstrations against the draft. In February of this year, a coalition was built to support Professor Harry Edwards' call to boycott a track meet held by the lily-white New York Athletic Club.

Two years ago, the Fort Hood Three Defense Committee arose to defend the rights of three GIs who refused to go to Vietnam. Because one of the GIs was an Afro-American, and another a Puerto Rican, nationalists and black-power advocates participated in the defense.

After the brutal attack on LeRoi Jones by Newark police during the rebellion last year, an Ad Hoc Committee of Afro-American Artists and Writers was formed. This committee's function was to raise funds for the legal defense of Jones and rally public support for him.

Specific purpose

All of the above united-front alliances and coalitions were established to fulfill a specific purpose or carry out a specific action. These alliances did not involve any attempt to gloss over the political and ideological differences of the participants.

Many times, white radicals and black militants confuse this single-issue or united-front type of alliance with a political or long-range type of alliance.

A case in point is the defense of Huey P. Newton. From a specific alliance to defend Newton, the Panther Party's working relationship with Peace and Freedom evolved into a political alliance that is supposed to aid in the liberation of the black nation.

A specific alliance with the Peace and Freedom Party to defend Newton is justifiable. In fact, each and every organization that is willing to defend Newton's constitutional rights, even if they do not agree with Newton's political views, should be incorporated in a legal-defense organization. Such a defense organization should include black liberals as well as white liberals. In this way, the task of raising funds and getting publicity would be made much easier.

In my opinion, the transformation of this specific alliance into a political or electoral alliance was a mistake. This was done, according to the Panther Party leadership, because the Peace and Freedom Party is a "revolutionary" organization.

Even if Peace and Freedom were revolutionary, it would still be a tactical question when and what type of working relationship should be established.

But evidence to justify such a characterization is almost nonexistent when you get down to the facts. The Peace and Freedom Party is a zoological collection of liberals and so-called white radicals. The party was able to meet ballot-status requirements in California by tapping anti-Johnson, antiwar sentiment without really winning people to any meaningful program.

As revealed by Peace and Freedom's national convention in Ann Arbor last month, Eldridge Cleaver's presidential campaign has been the major factor keeping the party from disintegrating. While the majority could agree on the nomination of Cleaver as their presidential candidate, none of the contesting factions could even agree on a vice-presidential candidate.

The Radical Caucus, one faction of the Peace and Freedom Party, is fighting for a program that comes down to verbal anticapitalism and support for the Cuban and Vietnamese Revolutions. The Independent Socialist Clubs, another faction, wants a milder program, such as fighting for reforms and limiting itself to such demands as bringing the GIs home now. The ISC, in an anticommunist stance, does not support either the Vietnamese or Cuban Revolutions.

After the California Peace and Freedom Party convention last March, Cleaver, disgusted, worked with the party through the Radical Caucus. After the national convention, Cleaver denounced both factions and moved toward the Youth International Party, the Yippies, which is not a part of the Peace and Freedom Party.

When it comes down to it, the Peace and Freedom Party is the worst electoral expression of white middle-class liberalism and faint-hearted radicalism.

North American capitalist society is divided into two nations, white America and black America, and into two main classes, the capitalist class and the working class.

It is obvious that the masses of Afro-America have radicalized in a manner that puts them far ahead of the white laboring masses. There is now the potential in the black community for building a powerful, mass black political party. Among white workers the situation is different. The masses of white workers have not radicalized to the point where the building of a mass labor party is possible. In no way can it be said that Peace and Freedom represents the beginnings of either a mass party of working people, or a vanguard socialist party which is organizing today to put together a party which can play a leading role in the future mass radicalization of the workers.

To categorize the Peace and Freedom Party, we have to place it programmatically between the parties of the capitalist exploiters and the vanguard parties of Afro-America and labor.

To dilly-dally in a political alliance with Peace and Freedom is to be diverted from the revolutionary highway into the swamp of middle-class politics. The building of a mass black political party cannot be achieved in a political coalition with Peace and Freedom. The Panthers have become a nationally known party because of their actions, not because of any association with Peace and Freedom. If the Panthers are to continue to grow, they need to cut the electoral strings tying them to this party.

While Panther Party leaders got involved at the Peace and Freedom convention in Ann Arbor, they did not intervene seriously at the Philadelphia Black Power Conference. Over 4,000 black people gathered together at this conference. Predominantly youthful, the thrust and sentiment was for the creation of an independent black political party. Participation by the national Panther leadership in the workshops and in the discussions would have made much headway in organizing this sentiment.

Instead of attending Peace and Freedom conventions, the BPP should be setting up Panther Party conventions. It would be better to run the political campaigns of Eldridge Cleaver, Bobby Seale, Kathleen Cleaver, and Huey Newton on a write-in basis rather than through Peace and Freedom. Electoral activity is only one of many activities along the path toward a revolutionary party.

It is hoped that this article has made some contribution to the understanding of alliances in building a black party.

Retreat from a Strategy of Mass Action
by Derrick Morrison

Last week we discussed the response of the Black Panther Party to the ruling-class efforts to wipe it out. We said that at the outset the Panther leadership had organized mass-action defense campaigns—the best examples being the 1968 Newton and Cleaver defense efforts. But later there followed a haphazard, hit-and-miss organization of defense, combined with profuse rhetoric about "picking up the gun," "the People will free Bobby," and "you can jail a revolutionary but you can't jail the revolution."

The evolution of the Panther defense policy is but a reflection of the Panther Party's attitude toward struggle in general.

At the time of the Newton and Cleaver defense campaigns, the Panthers were immersed in the task of organizing and educating masses of Black people around the struggle for self-determination. This was the case in terms of the Black student movement, the community self-defense campaigns, and to a certain degree in the electoral arena, which the Panthers were talking about entering to combat Black illusions about the Democratic Party.

But in each of these struggles, withdrawal occurred as soon as the Panthers confronted but found themselves unable to politically defeat the reformists, who seek to keep the masses fastened to the organizational machinery of the capitalist state.

In the case of the Black student movement, the Panther withdrawal began in January 1969. It was in this month that the Panther Party was engaged in struggle with Ron Karenga's US organization for leadership of the Black Student Union at UCLA. At issue was who would determine the shape of the Afro-American studies program slated for the campus. At the point that the Panthers were gaining the upper hand, the US organization assassinated two BSU leaders who were members of the Panther Party.

The Panthers couldn't respond militarily to this heinous act because that would have only played into the hands of the police, who were looking for an excuse to attack the Panther Party. The fact that the police were implicitly backing US created a relationship of forces that negated a response with arms.

The only other response possible was to embark upon a mass-action campaign of demonstrations, mass meetings, tribunals—both in and outside of the Black community—that would have politically isolated US.

But this incident seemed to paralyze the Panther Party, bringing to a halt its involvement in the campus struggle. Instead of waging a broad defense

---

Reprinted from the *Militant*, December 4, 1970

campaign that could have mobilized their many supporters, they lapsed into rhetorical positions of denouncing "cultural nationalism" in general with talk about "picking up the gun." Instead of seeking the widest possible support, they began to counterpose the community to the campus.

But in the Black community, the Panther Party's self-defense campaigns did not go very far. The reason lay in the inability of the party to go from education to the actual organization of united-front formations to mobilize other Black organizations and the masses of Black people against the occupation army in blue. Such a test—in the crucible of action—would have exposed reformists of all shades—Black Democrats and Republicans, poverty agents and Ford Foundation types. Thus the way would have been cleared for the rise of mass independent organizations in the Black community. The masses have to be convinced in action, not just by rhetoric, that they must go beyond reformism.

This lack of a strategy for community self-defense also characterized the moves by the Panther Party into the electoral arena. While talking about breaking Black people from the Democratic Party, the Panther Party actually hindered that effort by running electoral campaigns through the Peace and Freedom Party in 1968, rather than striking out independently and clearly posing the alternative of the Panther to the jackass and the elephant. The Peace and Freedom Party, composed of fainthearted white liberals and disoriented radicals, did not constitute a genuine break with capitalist politics.

Given these setbacks—in the student movement, the community, and the electoral arena—the Panther Party withdrew more and more from meaningful action into talk of armed struggle and "revolution."

What revolutionary-minded militants have to realize today is that revolution—a word thrown about very loosely—is nothing but uninterrupted *mass* action. This is the case in Vietnam, Palestine, and Cuba, where masses of people are thinking, acting, and organizing to take their destiny into their own hands.

To reach this uninterrupted stage of mass action in the United States, revolutionists must carry out the tasks of helping to build mass actions against the war in Vietnam to bring the troops home now, and mass actions by Blacks, Chicanos and Puerto Ricans to take control of their communities. These are the concrete issues on which people can be moved.

Pursuing these actions will give rise to mass independent parties in the Black, Puerto Rican and Chicano communities. And eventually, the working class as a whole—Black, Puerto Rican, Chicano, Asian-American, Native American and white—will see the need for independent, anticapitalist political action. Already, through actions against the war in Vietnam and for community control, Chicanos are realizing and organizing their independent strength through the Raza Unida Party in Texas and in Colorado.

These actions today, which go in a generally anticapitalist direction, but are not yet socialist in consciousness, are of a *transitional* character. The demands sparking and flowing out of these actions constitute what is known as a transitional program, a program designed to break the reformist illusions of the masses and begin to pose the need for a fundamental reorganization of society—to get rid of problems like war, racial and sexist oppression, and pollution.

The veering away of the Panther Party from the road of mass struggle was reflected in an article written by Huey P. Newton in the June 13 *Black Panther*. Written while he was in prison, it is entitled "Towards a New Constitution." The article contains the reasons for calling a Revolutionary People's Constitution Convention.

In it, Newton outlines the history of Black people in relation to capitalism.

After discussing the disenfranchisement and exploitation of Black people under capitalism, he concludes,

> We see that as far as autonomy of our community in any respect, as far as self-governing our institutions; this cannot exist under capitalism . . . because capitalism, the capitalistic system, is dictated by the small ruling class, approximately 76 companies that control the whole industry and the whole wealth of this country. That's General Motors, Ford, Chrysler, General Dynamics, Lockheed, Standard Oil, DuPont, Chase Manhattan Bank, Bank of America, and so on down the line.

> The only way that we can now get freedom is to change that system that led us into slavery.... We feel that the only way that we can get freedom at this time, after observing and experiencing the conditions of the country, is to have a Proportional Representation in a socialist framework. This means that the industries that now are held by a small ruling circle should be nationalized.

In respect to action, Newton writes that "any compromise" with the freedom of Black people is "suicidal."

Newton states further that compromise

> would be what I call reactionary suicide... Reactionary Suicide means that the conditions, the reactionary conditions, would be the cause of our suicide. If we stand and do nothing, it would be self-murder. I would rather choose the reverse, if it becomes necessary, and that is Revolutionary Suicide. That's suicide motivated by the desire to change the system, or else die trying. To change the reactionary conditions. But this is a freedom of choice. And I would choose this for the generation to come and I would choose it for my own integrity, for the simple reason that I refuse, our generation refuses, to live as slaves.

A rather lofty statement, but still a statement containing no prescription as to how to move in 1970, in the United States, a highly industrialized and urban terrain.

After all this talk about "revolutionary suicide," Newton writes, ". . . we are demanding a Constitution."

So outside of committing "revolutionary suicide," the Panthers offer the alternative of writing a new constitution!

A constitution changes when society changes. A revolutionary constitution comes after, not prior to, the social revolution. Twelve years after taking state power, the Cubans still don't have a constitution. This should give us an indication as to the relative importance of such a document.

But in any event, the masses of people in this country cannot relate to either "revolutionary suicide" or writing a new constitution. Neither alternative relates to the movement to end the Vietnam war, the fight for community control, or the struggle for women's liberation.

It is the growth and deepening of these key struggles that are helping to build the revolutionary vanguard party, the Socialist Workers Party. This is the case because none of the struggles mentioned above can be fought to completion under capitalism. Capitalism can't end imperialist wars; nor can it grant self-determination or abolish sexism. Thus, each struggle is imbued with an objectively anticapitalist dynamic, leading its participants to consciousness of this process and so advancing them into the revolutionary party.

Because the unreal alternatives of the Panthers—writing a new constitution or "revolutionary suicide"—amount to a negation of mass action, it is also a negation of what the Panthers claim to be seeking, namely, revolution.

Why Did the Black Panther Party Split?
by Tony Thomas

MARCH 29—In the April 3 *Militant*, we reported on the split in the Black Panther Party between supporters of Huey P. Newton and supporters of Kathleen and Eldridge Cleaver. Everyone concerned has recognized that this split and the personal charges and threats of physical violence between the factions are a setback for the Panthers.

While some people have been surprised with this "change" in the Black Panther Party (BPP), the split was the logical outcome of the past few years

Reprinted from the *Militant*, April 9, 1971

of the BPP's political development.

Recognition of the revolutionary dynamic of Black nationalism and the promotion of a program to mobilize and organize the Black community around its nationalist demands are the touchstone of revolutionary action in the Black community. It is the Panthers' failure to meet this test that provided the basis for their demise.

Potential of the Panthers

The Black Panther Party was started in 1966 by Huey Newton and Bobby Seale, who were students at Merritt College in Oakland, Calif. Eldridge Cleaver, who lived in San Francisco, joined shortly after it was launched.

During the initial period, they operated chiefly as a self-defense group in the Bay Area, protesting police brutality and supporting the right of Blacks to bear arms. It was during this period that they developed their 10-point program centered around Black control of the Black community.

This program was a good beginning toward the development of the kind of program that, if carried out through mass struggles for community control of the schools, police, and other institutions of the Black community, could have led to a big step forward for the Black struggle. The logic of such a struggle would have been a mass Black political movement independent of the Republican and Democratic parties.

The potential for such a party was shown in 1968 when the Panthers rapidly expanded on a nationwide scale, recruiting thousands of members and setting up dozens of chapters.

Political vacillations

Unfortunately, the leading cadres of the BPP were unequal to the task. Their main political characteristic was vacillation between ultraleftism and reformism.

They tended to overemphasize the armed aspects of the Black liberation struggle. In Huey P. Newton's pamphlet *The Correct Handling of a Revolution*, he talks about how the revolutionary movement of Afro-America would be sparked by armed bands of twos and threes, rather than mass mobilizations. In discussing the problem of self-defense, the Panthers seemed to feel that the technical aspects of armed struggle by their members were the key, rather than the mass organization of every segment of the Black community to both *politically* and physically defend the Black community.

In 1968, they had an opportunity to take a major step toward independent Black political action in the electoral arena, by running their own Black Panther candidates or supporting initiatives to launch a Black slate. Except in a few instances, the Panthers ran on and supported the national and local slates of the Peace and Freedom Party—a hodgepodge of radicals and liberals with a capitalist reform program.

The Panthers also failed to understand the necessity of carrying out united-front actions around such issues as opposition to the Vietnam war, Black community control, and Black studies with other groups in the Black community. This prevented them from undercutting and challenging the domination of reformist leaders and organizations in the Black community.

As their political disorientation deepened, ultraleft rhetoric about "picking up the gun," "Babylon," "revolutionary suicide," "intercommunalism," etc. became more and more of a substitute for a program of revolutionary nationalist action of a mass character. With such rhetoric, they were unable to relate to activists in Black community struggles who were initially attracted to the BPP by their self-defense orientation and 10-point program.

They began a whole series of maneuvers and gimmicks to take the place of a serious strategy and program for Black liberation.

'United Front Against Fascism'

A typical example was their United Front Against Fascism maneuver. In the spring of 1969, the Panthers discovered that "fascism" had already developed in the United States. They called for a conference of "all opposed to fascism," to meet in Oakland, Calif., July 18–21, 1969, to form a united "antifascist" front.

The Panthers' rhetoric about the existence of fascism was unable to mobilize more than a couple hundred Blacks, including Panthers, to attend the Oakland conference, though several thousand white radicals and liberals did attend. Instead of an open democratic conference, the UFAF conference was totally controlled by the Panthers, without any discussion from the floor. After all the ultraleft verbiage by the Panthers, the principal speakers at the conference were Black Democrats, pro-Democratic-Party Communist Party officials, and other reformists.

Almost everyone who attended the conference, except Black Panther and Communist Party members, felt that it was a failure. It called for no action except circulation of a petition for decentralization (Seale, in a motivating speech, said it would not be community control) of police. Even urgently needed discussion on building mass political defense of Black Panther political prisoners was ignored. Instead, a reformist political orientation was foisted on the nascent organization under the guise of combatting "fascism."

These ultraleft and reformist maneuvers became the standard feature of the Black Panther Party, which ceased to have any consistent program for Black liberation.

Leadership cult

None of these gyrations had anything to do with mobilizing Blacks in a fight independent of and in opposition to the Democratic and Republican parties around demands like the Panthers' own 10-point program.

Lacking a program with which to educate their membership, the Panthers attempted to build a cult of their leaders as superheroes to hold their organization together.

An example of this is indicated in an article by Bobby Seale in the April 20, 1969, *Black Panther* newspaper praising both Newton and Cleaver. Seale states: "Huey P. Newton and Eldridge Cleaver . . . are the two leading revolutionaries of our time. . . . With Eldridge Cleaver and Huey P. Newton, we have Lumumba and Malcolm X. . . . Our party can see Lenin and Stalin when we want to understand Huey and Eldridge. . . ." Later Seale puts Malcolm X in his place by quoting Cleaver, who said, "Malcolm X preceded Huey P. Newton like John the Baptist preceded Jesus Christ."

The Panthers made their decisions not on the basis of discussion on how to carry out a program by a membership politically educated on that program but on the basis of ultimatums of the Central Committee, which was responsible to nobody. This made it impossible and even dangerous for Panthers to correct or even explain policies that had proven inadequate in the struggle.

These problems were accentuated by the Panthers' pseudomilitary organizational methods and their attraction to Mao Tse-tung, Stalin, Kim Il Sung, and lately, Enver Hoxha of Albania. The rhetoric used by these Stalinist bureaucrats to justify their political maneuvers and political tyranny was adopted by the Black Panther's leaders to rationalize their own actions.

Fail to answer opponents

Lacking a consistent perspective, the Panthers were unable to explain their political differences with other groups within the Black liberation and radical movements except by castigating those with whom they disagreed as "counterrevolutionaries." An organization or individual was either "Part of the solution [with the Panthers] or part of the problem [against them]." This deadly sectarianism isolated them from other sections of the Black liberation movement and prevented them from leading or participating in united-front struggles.

Bobby Seale, in an Aug. 4, 1969, *Berkeley Barb* interview, attacked the criticisms of the Young Socialist Alliance and Socialist Workers Party concerning the United Front Against Fascism conference simply by saying, "We don't just relate to the Trotskyists as being our enemies . . . we see them as all being a part of the oppressive fascist power structure that's moving against all the revolutionary forces."

These methods of slander prevailed inside the BPP as well. In January 1969, the BPP announced that it had initiated a "national purge" and that they would refuse to accept new members for many months. Subsequently, the *Black Panther* was filled with "purge notices," with all types of personal and rhetorical insults on the "purged," but absolutely no mention of real political differences.

The March 9, 1969, *Black Panther* carried a typical purge notice, two lists of Panthers purged from the Oakland chapter. One stated, "The following persons are expelled from the Black Panther Party . . . and are thereby classified as Counterrevolutionaries." The other stated, "The following persons are expelled from the Black Panther Party. . . . They are thereby classified as renegades. . . ."

The April 20, 1969, *Black Panther* carried a notice that two Indiana Panthers had been purged because "Careful investigations found these two filthy-foul-mouthed renegade maggots at work in the treacherous ooze of their avaricious plotting. . . ."

Hundreds of people, whole chapters and regions, were expelled in this fashion. In the spring of 1969, there were three complete purges of the Detroit chapter, involving nearly the total membership each time.

The Panthers were also not opposed to using violence to settle differences within the movement. This was most concretely seen at the July 1969 United Front Against Fascism conference. Members of the Independent Socialist Club (now known as International Socialists), the Progressive Labor Party, and others who circulated leaflets critical of the Panthers were beaten by Panthers and their supporters.

Split not based on politics

Neither Cleaver's faction nor Newton's faction provides an answer for Black people. None of the criticism of the other by either of these groups goes beyond the political and organizational confusion that has led them to their current situation—a political and organizational confusion that was produced by the united effort of Cleaver, Seale, Newton, Hilliard, and the rest of the Panthers' leaders.

Only by repudiating this whole confusion can anyone attempt to find a way out for the Black liberation movement.

The Newtonites attack the Cleaver group for its refusal to defend Angela Davis, which is only a continuation of the basic sectarianism of the whole Black Panther Party. Newton, who began to disagree with Cleaver on the Davis defense when he recently split with him on organizational issues— has yet to come out for united-front actions in all spheres of defense and struggle, which is the only way to politically answer Cleaver's opposition to the Davis defense.

The Cleaverites attack Newton for acting like a superhero, but it was they themselves who participated in elevating Newton, Cleaver, and Seale to such positions.

Some people, such as the *San Francisco Good Times*, a Bay Area underground paper, claim that Newton represents a "right" wing as distinguished from Cleaver, who represents the "pick up the gun" wing of the BPP.

The facts are that both are responsible for the Panthers' zigs and zags in both directions. It was Cleaver who was the presidential candidate of the reformist Peace and Freedom Party. It was Newton who counterposed forming armed bands of twos and threes to mass action.

The answer to these problems is not primarily in criticizing the organizational moves made by both sides. The organizational life of a political group is related to and flows from its program.

The only answer is the repudiation of the political confusion and vacillation of the Panthers and the adoption of a strategy of mobilizing Black people to "control the institutions of their community," as Malcolm X put it. One of the most important opportunities for such struggle is a broad united effort to defend the Black Panther Party from the criminal attacks of the U.S. government. Another example of such an action is the Black Moratorium teach-in held in Highland Park, Mich., March 24, the Black antiwar actions called for April 2–5 in commemoration of Martin Luther King, and the continuing defense of the Black community of Cairo, Ill. Through the participation of Black revolutionaries in such struggles, a genuine mass Black political movement and the formation of a Black party will emerge.

Seale-Brown Campaign Steers Oakland Blacks Toward Democratic Party Swamp

by Rick Congress

OAKLAND—Bobby Seale and Elaine Brown, both national leaders of the Black Panther Party, are running in the local elections here. Seale is a candidate for mayor, and Brown is running for city council. The election is April 17. If no candidate gets a majority, a runoff will be held May 15.

The elections are officially "nonpartisan," but the party affiliations of all the candidates are known and publicized. The mayor, John Redding, a conservative Republican, is campaigning for another term. Otho Green, a Black business consultant, is a Democrat aligned with McGovern forces. Green is backed by the Oakland Democratic Black Caucus. John Sutter, a white liberal who is on the city council, has the support of the anti-McGovern Democrats.

Unfortunately, the Seale-Brown campaign offers no alternative to the capitalist parties in this election. Seale and Brown are campaigning as Democrats, not as Black Panther Party candidates. They are signing people up in the Democratic Party as part of their voter registration campaign.

By running as Democrats, Seale and Brown are asking Black people, workers and other oppressed people to support one of the parties responsible for maintaining capitalism, with its racism, wars, and exploitation. Thus their campaign leads in the wrong direction. It does not represent a step toward independent Black political action against the capitalist parties. Instead, it leads back into the swamp of Democratic Party politics.

The Black Panther Party has become more and more involved in coalition politics with the Democratic Party. In Berkeley, for example, it is supporting the April Coalition. This alliance between some radicals and a wing of the Democratic Party was put together to win votes on a liberal program. On a national level, it supported Black Democrat Shirley Chisholm in last year's Democratic Party primaries.

The campaign of Seale and Brown has evolved within this framework. An interview with Seale about his plans for the mayoralty campaign appeared in the September 1972 *Black Scholar*. Seale told the interviewer he wanted to "unify Black people around my mayoralty campaign simultaneously with our survival programs. The survival program is really a means of organizing Black people in the Black community."

He went on to say, "the main thing to do, of course, is to get the racist flunkies and lackeys of the capitalist ruling class out of the system."

In this interview, Seale seemed to project the Oakland campaign as a campaign of the Black Panther Party independent of the Democrats and Republicans.

But as their campaign progressed it became clear that Seale and Brown were not running as candidates of the Black Panther Party. They tried to get away from the image of a Black campaign, although it was precisely this aspect that was attractive to many Blacks. At first, they referred to themselves as "people's" candidates, or as "independents." But as the campaign grew more active, and in response to attacks on them for running against Black Democrat Otho Green, Seale and Brown began to campaign as Democrats.

They pasted up a strip reading "Democrat," on their original posters, which had no party designation. A new brochure was printed. It declared in bold type: "Elect two Democrats to public office." Their radio ads on the popular station in the Black community began to identify them as the "real effective Democrats."

This opportunistic capitulation to the Democratic Party reflected Seale and Brown's main objective in the campaign—to get themselves elected to office regardless of whether their campaign would aid or hinder the independent organization and mobilization of the Black community. They had been seriously talking about "a people's landslide" for Seale and Brown on April 17. But as it became increasingly obvious that this was not in the cards, they turned toward campaigning as Democrats in an effort to win more votes.

Reprinted from the *Militant*, April 13, 1973

This evolution of the campaign has caused controversy among many of their campaign supporters. The militant statements made at the beginning of the campaign attracted large numbers of young Blacks, primarily students, to the campaign. The Black Student Unions on the campuses in Oakland began functioning as Seale-Brown campaign committees. Several campaign rallies drew 300 to 400 young Black people.

During the early stages of the Seale-Brown campaign, before they began to campaign as Democrats, the Oakland Socialist Workers Party called for a vote for Seale and Brown as a means of furthering the development of independent Black political action against the capitalist parties. In this campaign Seale and Brown were—in the beginning—running against the Democrats and Republicans, although this was in contradiction to the Black Panther Party's national perspective of coalition politics with the Democrats.

Because the campaign was based in the Black community and was directed against the Democratic and Republican candidates, the SWP urged a vote for Seale and Brown, despite disagreement with them on a number of important questions.

In a public statement, James Lewis, SWP candidate for Oakland board of education, and Rick Congress, SWP candidate for Peralta Community College board of trustees, pointed out that by running against the Democratic and Republican candidates, Seale and Brown were objectively engaged in political action pointing toward a break by Black people with the parties of their oppressors. They cited the gains the Raza Unida parties in the Southwest made by organizing Chicanos in opposition to the capitalist parties as an example of the way forward for Black people too.

The SWP candidates criticized Seale and Brown for not using their campaign to explain the necessity of a political break with the Democratic Party. Lewis and Congress explained that the SWP's call for a vote for Seale and Brown was offered on the proviso that the campaign retain its independence from the Democrats and Republicans.

The SWP also pointed out that the Black Panther Party was making a mistake by not making a central part of the Seale-Brown campaign a projection of the need for a mass, independent Black party. This was further symbolized by their running as "independents" and not as Black Panther Party candidates.

Once Seale and Brown began to campaign as Democrats, the SWP reversed its call to vote for them. "By running as candidates of one of the parties of the ruling class," James Lewis explained,

> Seale and Brown are seriously misleading and miseducating the Black community about the possibility of achieving any improvement in the conditions of Black people through reliance on capitalist politics.
>
> The evolution of the Seale-Brown candidacies from formal independence from the Democrats and Republicans into Democratic candidacies reflects the basic pro-Democratic Party politics of the Black Panther Party.

Seale has justified his support for the Democratic Party by using the same excuses liberal Democrats offer: the Democratic Party is "where the people are," and it "can be reformed."

Seale is even described in the April 2 issue of *Newsweek* as "a perfectly respectable Democrat." He is quoted approvingly as explaining, "We want to turn Oakland into an all-American city."

Seale is now trying to outdo the two other Democratic candidates in pushing forward the Democratic Party label. The Seale-Brown campaign is thus misdirecting those people who were initially attracted to it on the strength of their support for independent Black political action. It is directing them right back into the trap of capitalist politics.

Oakland voters, however, still have an opportunity to vote against the capitalist and racist Democratic and Republican parties on April 17. They can do so by casting a ballot for the candidates of the Socialist Workers Party, James Lewis for Oakland board of education and Rick Congress for Peralta Community College board of trustees.

SECTION VIII. THE GARY CONVENTION

The National Black Political Convention held in Gary, Indiana, March 10–12, 1972, was attended by 8,000 delegates and observers from across the United States. It was the most significant and representative gathering held by the Black movement in decades. The convention adopted an agenda and a preamble that outlined a radical political perspective for the Black liberation struggle and contained a series of specific demands. Under the misleadership of the Congressional Black Caucus and other pro-Democratic Party forces, however, the convention failed to chart a course toward the formation of an independent Black political party, despite the wishes of a majority of the participants.

This section includes an article by Derrick Morrison appraising the convention reprinted from the pamphlet *Black Liberation and Political Power: The Meaning of the Gary Convention* (Pathfinder Press, 1972); the preamble to the National Black Agenda; and an analysis of the agenda by Tony Thomas, reprinted from the above pamphlet.

The Gary Convention and the Struggle for a Black Party
by Derrick Morrison

Despite a muted discussion and bureaucratic organization, the National Black Political Convention held March 10–12, 1972, in Gary, Indiana, reflected a new stage in the developing nationalist consciousness of Black people.

Up to now, the most vigorous examples of the organization of Black people as an oppressed nationality had been provided by Black students, Black GIs, Black prisoners, in some cases Black workers, and in a few cases Black women. But now even the Black Democratic Party politicians are reflecting the deepening discontent and nationalist sentiments of the Black community. Only a few years ago they denounced as "racism in reverse" all efforts at organizing Black people as a people; now they are legitimizing this concept on new levels.

From a position of trying to influence the policies of the capitalist parties—principally the Democratic Party—as individuals, they are now organizing as a group.

In 1969, for instance, Black state legislators formed a national organization called the Black Legislators Association. A year ago the thirteen Blacks in the House of Representatives formed the Congressional Black Caucus. Since then Black elected and appointed officials have been organizing caucuses on the local, county, and statewide level.

The ostensible purpose of these formations has been to bargain for concessions from the Democratic and Republican parties. The Congressional Black Caucus and other Black politicians saw the National Black Political Convention as a device to extract more meaningful concessions from the Democratic and Republican national conventions than they had been able to obtain in the past.

This bolder approach by the Black politicians draws its strength from two sources: the increasing number of Black elected and appointed officials and the nationalist radicalization of Black people. The first is actually a product of the second, but it deserves singling out.

In 1967, prior to the election of Richard G.

Hatcher as mayor of Gary and the election of Carl B. Stokes to the same position in Cleveland, Blacks held fewer than 480 of the 522,000 public offices in the U.S. As of the spring of 1971, Blacks held 1,860 positions, nearly a fourfold increase.

The nationalist radicalization grows out of the racist oppression suffered by Black people at the hands of American capitalist society. It was sparked by the post–World War II outbreak of national liberation struggles in Africa, Asia, and Latin America, and it issued directly from the civil rights movement of the 1960s. The urbanization of Black people, combined with the inability of American capitalism to solve the mounting problems of the cities, fuels this nationalist consciousness. According to the February 11, 1971, *New York Times*, close to 9.1 million Black people occupied the central cities in 1960. The 1970 census reported an increase to nearly 12.5 million.

Black unemployment has become alarmingly high. With the official national rate for overall unemployment running around 6 percent, unemployment for Black teen-agers in "urban poverty neighborhoods" has reached the staggering figure of 45 percent.

Federal funding of antipoverty programs is down. Cutbacks are being made in every aspect of services provided by city and state governments. Even the Ford Foundation, which has funded a number of projects in the Black community, is cutting back to the lowest level of grant-making since 1961.

Moreover, in accord with the maxim of being "last hired and first fired," many Black people hired in the late 1960s under the impact of the civil rights agitation and the ghetto rebellions are now being turned out on the streets.

The wage controls Nixon inaugurated last August come on top of the vast unemployment and government cutbacks. Combined with the rampant spread of drugs and the multitude of other problems confronting the ghetto, these factors are producing a marked deterioration in the quality of Black life—which wasn't too high in the first place.

This deterioration is deepening the awareness of Black people that the racist capitalist government cannot and will not solve the problems of the Black community. This in turn pushes the Black politicians to adopt militant and nationalist rhetoric in order to justify their position in the two capitalist parties—especially the Democrats—and to maintain Black support for those parties.

This new stance was expressed in the National Black Agenda, the platform adopted by the Gary convention. It was also presented in the addresses to the convention by Gary mayor Richard Hatcher and the Reverend Jesse Jackson, head of Operation PUSH (People United to Save Humanity).

Hatcher and Jackson gave the only speeches to the 8,000 delegates and observers. Both of them gestured toward the next stage of the Black struggle: the organization of a Black party in opposition to the Democrats and Republicans.

The remarks by Hatcher and Jackson derive their importance not only from what they may or may not be thinking as individuals, but from the fact that they represent what growing numbers of Black people are willing to consider. Hatcher and Jackson reflect the pressures from below. Hundreds of thousands of Black people are no longer automatically granting support to the two capitalist parties.

The organization of all-Black caucuses and factions by the politicians and the holding of the Gary convention have made many Black people less hesitant about the idea of a Black party. For if all of this motion can go into just extracting a few more crumbs from the Democratic Party, then why can't the Rubicon be crossed and a convention called to set up a party for, by, and of Black people? This is the task of the hour.

Then why didn't the convention form such a party? The main reason lies with the firm grip those Black politicians committed to the Democratic Party had on the convention. But these politicians got plenty of aid from the organized Black nationalist groups that came to Gary.

The major nationalist groups that participated in the convention—Congress of African People, Congress of Racial Equality, Republic of New Africa, Black Panther Party, the Student Organization for Black Unity and the Washington, D.C., Black United Front—are on record as supporters and advocates of organizing a Black party.

The Congress of African People (CAP) figured prominently at Gary, and one of its national leaders, Imamu Amiri Baraka (LeRoi Jones), was designated one of the three convention cochairmen. CAP not only supports the formation of a Black party in the U.S., but calls for a "World African Party." Baraka, as chairman of the political liberation council of CAP, has spelled out this concept in a number of articles and speeches.

The Student Organization for Black Unity (SOBU), a national organization based primarily in the South, has helped initiate a fledgling Black party in North Carolina called the Black People's Union Party.

The March 7, 1972, *New York Times* reported the Reverend Doug Moore of the D.C. Black United Front as saying that the nationalists would push for the formation of a national Black party at the convention.

Besides these formal positions of the nationalist organizations in support of a Black party, other formations and individuals either agitated for or issued statements endorsing the concept. For instance, the Reverend Jackson indicated for the first time his support of the concept in his convention address.

And a couple of weeks before the convention, Bryant Rollins, executive editor of the New York *Amsterdam News*—an influential Black weekly whose circulation is second only to *Muhammad Speaks*—stressed the idea that the convention should form a national Black party.

Why didn't the nationalist delegates mobilize this sentiment, give it program and direction, and struggle at the convention for its implementation?

The answer to this question lies in the illusions these nationalists developed in respect to the Gary convention. They thought that by subordinating their positions on a Black party to the preservation of "unity" with the Congressional Black Caucus and other Black Democratic Party politicians, they were contributing to the process of building the political power of Black people. So they sought support on tangential issues.

Baraka and CAP sought endorsement of their proposal for a National Black Political Assembly. CORE sought support for opposition to busing Black students to white schools in favor of Black community control of the schools. The Republic of New Africa proposed that the convention demand freedom for its activists jailed in Jackson, Mississippi, and support the RNA-sponsored plebiscites in the South to establish a Black state.

The Panthers wanted endorsement of their "survival" programs providing free food, clothing, and other commodities in the Black community. The D.C. Black United Front introduced a resolution supporting the right of the Palestinian Arabs to self-determination and calling for the dismantling of the Zionist settler-state of Israel. SOBU requested support for the projected May 27, 1972, national demonstration in solidarity with the African revolution.

All of these proposals were passed with no break in "unity." But the fact that this "unity" was based upon submerging the question of the Black party became quite clear when nationalists leading the Louisiana delegation put a resolution on the floor calling for such a party. None of the delegates who are members of the major nationalist groups mentioned above rose to support and defend the resolution. Baraka, who was chairing the convention session at the time, tried to avoid it.

When the Louisiana delegates persisted, Baraka opened discussion. The resolution was successfully pigeon-holed, however, with the aid of the Illinois and Indiana delegations. The Reverend Jackson, who spoke for Illinois, clinched the operation with the argument that the Black Assembly would inevitably lead to the realization of a Black party. The Louisiana delegates broke out in applause upon hearing this and withdrew their resolution.

As outlined by CAP, the National Black Assembly would be composed of 427 Blacks, ranging from politicians to community activists. It would serve as a "focal point of Black politics in the United States, moving to a more concrete relationship with our brothers and sisters on the (African) continent," according to Baraka in the March 13, 1972, *Washington Post*. Moreover, "it would be a chief brokerage operation for dealing with the white power political institutions [read Democratic and Republican parties]." So the chief function of the Assembly is to operate as a pressure group upon the two capitalist parties.

The more than 3,000 delegates endorsed the proposal. But does the Black Assembly, as some have been led to believe, actually represent the beginnings of an independent Black party? There is nothing wrong with pressuring the two capitalist parties for concessions. But the operation of the Black Assembly, while giving the appearance of independence, is contingent upon endorsing the politics of the Black Democratic Party politicians, which is only another way of becoming hooked to the Democratic Party. This is the real meaning of the "unity" at Gary.

Baraka and the Newark CAP have already borne out this logic. Ever since the election of Newark mayor Kenneth Gibson in 1970, Baraka and his followers have submerged themselves in Democratic Party politics. They are now preparing for the national convention of the Democratic Party in Miami next July. Moreover, since the Gary convention, some of the nationalist groups in New York City have begun preparations along the same line.

Contrary to what Baraka and other like-minded nationalists think, political independence does not begin in the Democratic Party, but outside of it, in opposition to it. They will not be able to use the party of the oppressor to build the power of the oppressed. By refusing to mobilize Black people's political strength for themselves, in a party of, by, and for Black people, they are in fact continuing the utilization of that strength to augment the political power of the white capitalist oppressor. So the formation of the Black Assembly is hardly a step toward independence.

This is not say that nationalists should not attempt to achieve *unity in action* around specific issues with the Black Democratic Party politicians, or Black Republican Party politicians for that matter. For a specific action, such as the May 27 African Liberation Day or in the defense of the jailed RNA activists, support should be sought from all Blacks, whatever their political persuasion. For example, in the Chicano liberation movement, many Chicano nationalists have built powerful actions against the war in Southeast Asia, against police brutality in the Chicano community, and in defense of democratic rights for victimized Chicanos. And they have involved Chicanos of all political opinions. But when it comes to the question of power, i.e. political control of the community, that's where some Chicano nationalists have drawn the line with Chicanos in the Democratic Party.

Since Chicanos do not control the Democratic Party, and since they see that party bearing a lot of the responsibility for oppressing the Chicano community, Chicano nationalists have created their own party—La Raza Unida Party. This independent Chicano party is active in Texas, Colorado, and California. And where this party exists, Chicanos are beginning to utilize their political strength on their own behalf. They are opposing the rule of the Democratic and Republican parties at the ballot box as well as in the streets.

Black people have a lot of political strength. That's why the Democratic Party politicians work so hard at keeping that strength operating on behalf of the Democratic Party. However, Black people have already organized to utilize their political strength in their own interests—on the campuses, in the high schools, in the military, in the prisons, and on the job in some cases. This is where mass opposition has been displayed to the policies and programs of the Democratic and Republican parties. The next stage of the struggle—which the Gary convention pointed to but did not actually mount—is the generalization of this process of independent organization into the electoral arena by the formation of a Black party.

This is the conclusion many Black people have already drawn. As the present set of illusions about the nature of the Democratic and Republican parties wear out, many more will be pushed in that direction. The next time a Black convention is held, the chances are that a real discussion will take place on the need to embark on an independent course.

Preamble to the National Black Political Agenda

What time is it?

We come to Gary in an hour of great crisis and tremendous promise for Black America. While the white nation hovers on the brink of chaos, while its politicians offer no hope of real change, we stand on the edge of history and are faced with an amazing and frightening choice: We may choose in 1972 to slip back into the decadent white politics of American life or we may press forward, moving relentlessly from Gary to the creation of our own Black life. The choice is large but the time is very short.

Let there be no mistake. We come to Gary in a time of unrelieved crisis for our people. From every rural community in Alabama to the high-rise compounds of Chicago, we bring to this Convention the agonies of the masses of our people. From the sprawling Black cities of Watts and Nairobi in the West to the decay of Harlem and Roxbury in the East, the testimony we bear is the same. We are witnesses to social disaster.

Our cities are crime-haunted dying grounds. Huge sectors of our youth—and countless others—face permanent unemployment. Those of us who work find our paychecks able to purchase less and less. Neither the courts nor the prisons contribute to anything resembling justice or reformation. The schools are unable—or unwilling—to educate our children for the real world of our struggles. Meanwhile, the officially approved epidemic of drugs threatens to wipe out the minds and strength of our best young warriors.

Economic, cultural, and spiritual depression stalk Black America, and the price for survival often appears to be more than we are able to pay. On every side, in every area of our lives, the American institutions in which we have placed our trust are unable to cope with the crises they have created by their single-minded dedication to profits for some and white supremacy above all.

Beyond these shores

And beyond these shores there is more of the same. For while we are pressed down under all the dying weight of a bloated, inwardly decaying white civilization, many of our brothers in Africa and the rest of the Third World have fallen prey to the same powers of exploitation and deceit. Wherever America faces the unorganized, politically powerless forces of the non-white world, its goal is domination by any means necessary—as if to hide from itself the crumbling of its own systems of life and work.

But Americans cannot hide. They can run to China and the moon and to the edges of consciousness, but they cannot hide. The crises we face as Black people are the crises of the entire society. They go deep, to the very bones and marrow, to the essential nature of America's economic, political, and cultural systems. They are the natural end product of a society built on the twin foundations of white racism and white capitalism.

So, let it be clear to us now: The desperation of our people, the agonies of our cities, the desolation of our countryside, the pollution of the air and the water—these things will not be significantly affected by new faces in the old places in Washington, D.C. This is the truth we must face here in Gary if we are to join our people everywhere in the movement forward toward liberation.

White realities, Black choice

A Black political convention, indeed all truly Black politics must begin from this truth: *The American system does not work for the masses of our people, and it cannot be made to work without radical fundamental change.* [Emphasis in original—*ISR*] (Indeed, this system does not really work in favor of the humanity of anyone in America.)

In the light of such realities, we come to Gary and are confronted with a choice. Will we believe the truth that history presses into our face—or will we, too, try to hide? Will the small favors some of us have received blind us to the larger sufferings of our eyes to the testimony of our history in America?

For more than a century we have followed the path of political dependence on white men and their systems. From the Liberty Party in the de-

---

Reprinted from *International Socialist Review*, May 1972

cades before the Civil War, to the Republican Party of Abraham Lincoln, we trusted in white men and white politics as our deliverers.

Sixty years ago, W.E.B. Du Bois said he would give Woodrow Wilson and the Democrats their "last chance" to prove their sincere commitment to equality for Black people—and he was given white riots and official segregation in peace and in war.

Nevertheless, some twenty years later, we became Democrats in the name of Franklin Roosevelt, then supported his successor Harry Truman, and even tried a "non-partisan" Republican General of the Army named Eisenhower. We were wooed like many others by the superficial liberalism of John F. Kennedy and the make-believe populism of Lyndon Johnson. Let there be no more of that.

Both parties have betrayed us

Here at Gary, let us never forget that while the times and the names and the party have continually changed, one truth has faced us insistently, never changing: Both parties have betrayed us whenever their interests conflicted with ours (which was most of the time), and whenever our forces were unorganized and dependent, quiescent and compliant.

Nor should this be surprising, for by now we must know that the American political system, like all other white institutions in America, was designed to operate for the benefit of the white race: It was never meant to do anything else.

That is the truth that we must face at Gary. If white "liberalism" could have solved our problems, then Lincoln and Roosevelt and Kennedy would have done so. But they did not solve ours nor the rest of the nation's. If America's problems could have been solved by forceful, politically skilled, and aggressive individuals, then Lyndon Johnson would have retained the presidency. If the true "American Way" of unbridled monopoly capitalism, combined with a ruthless military imperialism could do it, then Nixon would not be running in panic around the world, or making speeches comparing his nation's decadence to that of Greece and Rome.

If we have never faced it before, let us face it at Gary: The profound crisis of Black people and the disaster of America are not simply caused by men, nor will they be solved by men alone.

These crises are the crises of basically flawed economics and politics, and of cultural degradation. None of the Democratic candidates and none of the Republican candidates—regardless of their vague promises to us or to their white constituencies—can solve our problems or the problems of this country without radically changing the systems by which it operates.

The politics of social transformation

So we come to Gary confronted with a choice. But it is not the old convention question of which candidate shall we support, the pointless question of who is to preside over a decaying and unsalvageable system.

No, if we come to Gary out of the realities of the Black communities of this land, then the only real choice for us is whether or not we will live by the truth we know, whether we will move to organize independently, move to struggle for fundamental transformation, for the creation of new directions, towards a concern for the life and the meaning of Man. Social transformation or social destruction, those are our only real choices.

If we have come to Gary on behalf of our people in America, in the rest of this hemisphere, and in the Homeland—if we have come for our own best ambitions—then a new Black Politics must come to birth. If we are serious, the Black Politics of Gary must accept major responsibility for creating both the atmosphere and the program for fundamental, far-ranging change in America. Such responsibility is ours because it is our people who are most deeply hurt and ravaged by the present systems of society.

That responsibility for leading the change is ours because we live in a society where few other men really believe in the possibility of a truly humane society for anyone anywhere.

We are the vanguard

The challenge is thrown to us here in Gary. *It is the challenge to consolidate and organize our own Black role as the vanguard in the struggle for a new society.* [Emphasis in original—*ISR*] To accept that challenge is to move to independent Black politics. There can be no equivocation on that issue. History leaves us no other choice. White politics has not and cannot bring the changes we need.

We come to Gary and are faced with a challenge. The challenge is to transform ourselves from favor-seeking vassals and loud-talking, "militant" pawns, and to take up the role that the unorganized masses of our people have attempted to play ever since we came to these shores, that of harbingers of true justice and humanity, leaders in the struggle for liberation.

A major part of the challenge we must accept is that of redefining the functions and operations of all levels of American government, for the existing governing structures—from Washington to the smallest county—are obsolescent. That is part of the reason why nothing works and why corruption rages throughout public life. For white politics seeks not to serve but to dominate and manipulate.

We will have joined the true movement of history if at Gary we grasp the opportunity to press Man forward as the first consideration of politics. Here at Gary we are faithful to the best hopes of our fathers and our people if we move for nothing less than a politics which places community before individualism, love before sexual exploitation, a living environment before profits, peace before war, justice before unjust "order", and morality before expediency.

This is the society we need, but we delude ourselves here at Gary if we think that change can be achieved without organizing the power, the determined national Black power, which is necessary to insist upon such change, to create such change, to seize change.

Towards a Black agenda

So when we turn to a Black Agenda for the seventies, we move in the truth of history, in the reality of the moment. We move recognizing that no one else is going to represent our interests but ourselves. *The society we seek cannot come unless Black people organize to advance its coming.* [Emphasis in original—*ISR*] We lift up a Black Agenda recognizing that white America moves towards the abyss created by its own racist arrogance, misplaced priorities, rampant materialism, and ethical bankruptcy. Therefore we are certain that the Agenda we now press for in Gary is not only for the future of Black humanity, but is probably the only way the rest of America can save itself from the harvest of its criminal past.

So, Brothers and Sisters of our developing Black nation, we now stand in Gary as a people whose time has come. From every corner of Black America, from all liberation movements of the Third World, from the graves of our fathers and the coming world of our children, we are faced with a challenge and a call: Though the moment is perilous we must not despair. We must seize the time, for the time is ours.

We begin here and now in Gary. We begin with an independent Black political movement, an independent Black Political Agenda, an independent Black spirit. Nothing less will do. We must build for our people. We must build for our world. We stand on the edge of history. We cannot turn back.

The Meaning of the Black Political Agenda
by Tony Thomas

The National Black Agenda passed at the March 10–12 National Black Political Convention held in Gary, Indiana, marks an important step toward codifying a program for the struggle for Black liberation. The Black Agenda charts a course aimed at Black control of the major social, economic, and educational institutions in the Black community. The Agenda has an added significance because it was approved by an overwhelming majority at the National Black Political Convention. It is a barometer of the strengths and weaknesses of large sectors of the Black liberation movement.

The National Black Political Convention was one of the most significant gatherings of Black people in many years. It was attended by 8,000 delegates and observers, including representatives of community organizations, nationalist groups, and student organizations, as well as welfare-rights activists, union officials, poverty program functionaries, and Democratic and Republican party politicians and officials.

The size and breadth of the conference signify a new awareness of the electoral arena and its potential use for building Black political power. More and more African-Americans are realizing that the current policies and leadership of the Democratic and Republican parties are tied to a program of oppression of Black people. More and more Black people are realizing that the struggle to control their communities cannot be won without the struggle for political power.

The conference at Gary was organized by Black Democratic politicians such as Michigan Congressman Charles Diggs and other members of the Congressional Black Caucus, and by Black nationalists and Pan-Africanists such as Imamu Amiri Baraka (LeRoi Jones) of the Congress of African People. They did not aim to organize a Black political movement that would be independent of the Democratic and Republican parties. They did not aim to organize mass actions around the demands of the Black community. Instead, they aimed to utilize the conference to put pressure on the leaders of the Democratic Party from within the Democratic Party.

The conference essentially went along with this perspective. Baraka and the Black Democrats found it expedient to apply the rhetoric of opposition to the Democratic and Republican parties, and the rhetoric of Black control of the Black community. But the leaders of the conference prevented any type of serious democratic discussion of these issues by the elected delegates.

Richard Hatcher, Democratic mayor of Gary, claimed that he was giving the Democrats their "last chance" in the 1972 elections. He said that he supported a break from the Democrats sometime in the future, and that he favored independent political action by Puerto Ricans, Chicanos, Native Americans, students, and workers as well as Blacks. Another leader of the convention, Rev. Jesse Jackson, leader of PUSH (People United to Save Humanity) urged the construction of a Black party (again in the future) while at the same time urging the convention to seek "delegate power" at the Democratic convention.

The Black Agenda was presented at the conference as an attempt to give a militant nationalist cover to the conservative strategy of working within the Democratic Party. The Agenda advocated in *words* the sentiments of masses of Afro-Americans, while the conference endorsed in deeds a strategy of Black involvement—through caucuses and factions—in the Democratic Party. The Agenda is a reflection of the pressure of the radicalized nationalist sentiment in the Black community on Baraka and the Congressional Black Caucus.

The Agenda was forthright enough, however, to draw fire from moderate Black organizations—before, during, and after the Gary convention. In a memorandum written before the convention to members of the National Association for the Advancement of Colored People who were delegates at the Black Convention, NAACP Assistant Executive Director John A. Morsell claimed the Agenda was "not an acceptable document for the NAACP" because it was "rooted in the concept of separate nationhood for Black Americans." Morsell attacked it for calling for "withdrawal from the American political process on the thesis that this is 'white' politics."

The NAACP memorandum said of the preamble that the Agenda's "rhetoric is that of revolution rather than of reform, although we note that it stops short of its logical conclusion, which is revolt aimed at setting up a new nation with its own territorial base."

During the convention, the majority of the Michigan delegation walked out because they found the Agenda "too militant." This group was dominated by antinationalist delegates from organizations like the NAACP, and representatives of the AFL-CIO and United Auto Workers' bureaucracies. After the walkout, leaders of the delegation told this writer that their principal fear was that passage of the Black Political Agenda would endanger their links with the Democratic Party in Michigan and nationally.

When the Michigan delegates voiced their dissatisfaction at the Gary convention, Imamu Amiri Baraka, Rev. Jesse Jackson, and other leaders of the convention told them that the Agenda was only a draft. This was despite a previous decision by the convention to endorse it. Later it was announced that a "final" version of the Black Political Agenda would be made public on May 19. This "final" version was to be drawn up by a steering committee of heads of the state delegations at the convention. It was assured that this version would be more palatable to the Michigan delegation and other more conservative forces within the Black movement.

In a statement reported in the March 23, 1972, *New York Times*, the Congressional Black Caucus and Mayor Richard Hatcher repudiated the position taken by the convention to support the Palestinian struggle and oppose the Zionist State of Israel. Similar attacks were leveled by moderates on the position taken in the Agenda and at the convention on busing.

The Black Political Agenda, which was the center of this controversy, may now be deliberately hidden, or watered down by the pro-Democratic Party organizers of the Gary convention. Nevertheless, it remains an important indicator of the ideas circulating in large sectors of the Black liberation struggle.

Despite setbacks suffered by the Black liberation struggle, such as the decimation of the Black Panther Party, the Black nationalist radicalization has deepened within the Black community in recent years.

American capitalism has been unable to solve the basic problems facing the Black community: unemployment, poverty, drugs, police brutality, political repression, and the lack of decent educational, health, recreational, and cultural facilities. In fact, with the present attack on the standard of living of the entire population (Nixon's "New Economic Policy"), the conditions facing Afro-Americans are getting worse. As the document points out: "We are witnesses to social disaster."

The Agenda charts a Black nationalist course of self-reliance. It refers to Afro-Americans as a Black Nation and states: ". . . no one else is going to represent our interests but ourselves. *The society we seek cannot come unless Black people organize to advance its coming.*" (Emphasis in original.)

The goal is to be achieved through a mass movement for Black control. In the section entitled "The Direction" following the preamble, the Agenda states:

The Black politics we need goes far beyond electoral politics and far beyond 1972. *We need a permanent political movement that addresses itself to the basic control and reshaping of American institutions that currently exploit Black America and threaten the whole society.* The unifying objective of this political movement must be the empowerment of the Black community, not simply its representatives. It must offer basic alternatives to all existing American political, economic and cultural systems. (Emphasis in original.)

The Black Political Agenda proposes Black control of the Black community and the institutions affecting it. In the section on economics, the Agenda demands the establishment through federal funds of a "Black development agency . . . under Black leadership and control for the purpose of facilitating Black ownership and/or control of the full range of business and service enterprises now serving ghetto communities, including public transportation and communication systems, day care and health centers, housing, educational and commercial and financial institutions."

On education, the Agenda demands: "The development of mechanisms for Black control of the schools where Black children are educated, moving beyond the sterile issue of 'busing' to the basic issue of the redistribution of educational wealth and control." This view was reflected by the decision of the convention which stated the issue was not only busing but Black control over education and the allotment of adequate funds to finance decent education for Black children. In addition the convention endorsed the right of Blacks to utilize busing programs for immediate educational gains.

On the prisons the Agenda supported the demands for a prisoners' bill of rights and added that it advocated: ". . . the establishment of local community control over the courts and the prisons." The Agenda further demanded: "the establishment of local control over the police and the establishment of residency requirements for all neighborhood police forces."

In addition to these demands for community control, the Agenda made a series of further demands for democratic rights for Afro-Americans and for improvement in the economic and social conditions of Black people.

The Agenda demanded proportional representation for Black people within the U.S. Congress, calling for fifteen Black senators and sixty-six Black representatives to be elected at-large by the Black community. The Agenda also stated, "The same principle shall obtain for state and local governments."

The Agenda called for billions of dollars in reparations for the hundreds of years of exploitation Black people have faced. It added that "full economic development for us cannot take place without radical transformation of the economic system." It raised the demand for a $5,200 minimum guaranteed income for a family of four and a minimum wage of $2.50 per hour. It demanded "free public transportation"; abolition of taxes on incomes under $10,000 a year; establishment of "free public education for all Black people up to their highest attainable level"; free medical care for families with an income under $10,000; withdrawal by the U.S. government of "all corporations, military bases, communications facilities and other institutions which contribute to the dehumanization or subjugation of African and Third World peoples"; and Black control over a proportionate number of radio and TV stations.

These are the type of demands that reflect the problems and interests of the masses of Black people. Many of these demands have already been raised in struggles for community control, in struggles of Black workers, welfare activists, and students. The Agenda proposes that the resources of this society be utilized to meet the educational, social, cultural, and economic needs of the Black community rather than the profits of "white capitalism."

American capitalism cannot by any stretch of the imagination grant most of these demands. Without the disparity in wages between Blacks and whites, big business would lose billions of dollars of profit. More billions would be lost if financial resources were diverted to provide adequate social, educational, and health services for Afro-Americans. Still more billions would be lost if the imperialists ended their exploitative operations in Africa, Asia, and Latin America as the Black Agenda advocates.

Furthermore, if these demands were raised by a mass movement for Black liberation other social forces exploited and oppressed by U.S. capitalism, facing many of the same problems, would be pressed into action. Already Chicanos, Puerto Ricans, Asians, and Native Americans have raised similar demands. Nixon's wage freeze has attacked the standard of living not only of Afro-Americans but of all working people in the United States.

As the Black Agenda states several times, these demands can only be gained by replacing the system. They run directly against the interests and desires of the big industrialists and financiers who control the Democratic and Republican parties. The Agenda reflects the growing hostility of Black people at the do-nothing politics of these parties:

> Both parties have betrayed us whenever their interests conflicted with ours (which was most of the time). . . . Nor should this be surprising, for by now we must know that the American political system, like all other white institutions in America, was designed to operate for the benefit of the white race . . .

The problems of Black people, according to the Black Political Agenda, "will not be significantly affected by new faces in the old places in Washington, D. C." Instead, "To accept that challenge is to move to independent Black politics."

Despite these attacks on the Republican and Democratic parties and a call for an "independent Black Political movement," the Black Agenda contains no concrete program of action for gaining the demands it raises. This is the most significant weakness of the Agenda.

The only thing approaching a concrete step to be taken in the political arena is a proposal that Black youth be organized through "a national voter education and registration drive and the formation of a national Black political pressure and action group . . ." The Agenda calls for a "Black Youth Lobby" to do this pressuring.

Rather than pressuring, a definitive break from the Republican and Democratic parties is needed if Black people are to reach the goals set in the Black Agenda. This weakness is consistent, despite the anti-Democratic Party statements, with the Black Convention's continued support to working within and pressuring the Democratic and Republican parties.

One proposal raised by the Louisiana delegation to the Gary Convention was the idea of a Black political party independent of, and in opposition to, the Democrats and Republicans. This proposal was the logical culmination of the demands and sentiments expressed by the Black Agenda—that Black people control the politics and institutions of the Black community.

This proposal was hustled off the floor by the convention leaders. Rev. Jesse Jackson speaking on this issue claimed that the "Black political movement is too young" for such an effort. Others argued that the proposal would disrupt the "unity" of the convention. However, no one was willing to openly reject the proposal for a Black party; instead, it was decided to submit this proposal to the steering committee for future consideration.

The fact that the leaders of the convention were unable to openly oppose the creation of a Black party shows the ripeness within the Black community for such a party.

Although Black elected and appointed officials, almost all Democrats, increased from 480 (out of 522,000) in the spring of 1967 to 1,860 in the spring of 1971, no substantial improvements have been made in the living conditions of masses of Black people.

In Newark, New Jersey, and Gary, Indiana, the two largest cities controlled by Black Democratic administrations, no substantial gains have been made toward solving these problems. While massive Black votes have elected these administrations, the Black Democratic mayors must stay within the limitations set by the Democratic party. As the Black Agenda pointed out, these limitations mean staying within a system that is based on the oppression of Black people.

A Black political party, on the other hand, would be a realistic way of solving the conditions of political powerlessness faced by the Black community. The idea of Black "unity" was mentioned often at the Black Convention. But real Black political unity—that is, in the interests of the masses of Black people—can only take place when Black people have their own political party. To claim that a proposal for a Black party disrupts Black unity, is to claim that the only type of unity required is unity based on submission to the enemies of the Black nation.

A Black political party, on the other hand, would not be bound by such submission; rather it would be based on the needs and desires of the Afro-American people. Demands for community control and improvement of the basic living conditions of the Black community such as those in the Black Agenda would be the center of its campaigns.

Rather than relying on pressuring the racist capitalist parties or getting a Black person into office under these parties, a Black political party would capitalize on the rise in Black political consciousness to win political power for Black people.

Moreover, a Black political party, unlike the Democratic Party would seek to mobilize Afro-Americans for struggles outside of the electoral arena. As the *Case for a Black Party*, a resolution passed by the 1967 convention of the Socialist Workers Party, stated:

> A political party based on the ghetto could carry out many worthwhile activities in addition to running for or holding political offices. It could conduct education about Black history and revolutionary struggles elsewhere; take measures to form cooperatives and credit systems to ease the economic squeeze; defend Black victims of government persecution; initiate literacy campaigns among adults; organize Afro-American cultural affairs and community recreation. Its contests for control of legitimate authority would give it much more leverage in fights against landlords, brutal cops, and job discrimination. It could organize neighborhood patrols against crime and rackets and demand an end to the alien and repressive police powers of racist rulers. It could provide a broad framework for unifying various Black groups in common struggle. (New York: Pathfinder Press, p. 11.)

The struggle for Black political power lies not only through electoral activities, but through mass actions. A Black political party, unlike even the most "progressive" Democrats, could unify and coordinate these two indispensable aspects of the fight for Black liberation.

Linked to the absence of a call for a Black party, still another weakness of the Agenda is that it did not call for mass actions and struggles to gain the demands it raises. Mass actions around these demands can heighten the political consciousness and organization of the Black community. Rent strikes; welfare-rights actions; actions by Black workers, Black students, and Black GIs form a powerful complement to the movement for Black control of the Black community and Black political power, and quicken the pace of the march toward a Black political party.

It is around such actions that diverse forces in the Afro-American struggle can be involved in united action, and the different programs and strategies within the movement can be tested against each other in action. An example of such actions are the recent Children's March on Washington and the upcoming May 27 African Solidarity demonstrations scheduled for Washington and San Francisco.

Without either a call for a Black party, or even a call for mass actions to gain its demands, the Black Agenda can be interpreted as a set of goals for the hazy and distant future, rather than a program for struggle right now.

For activists within the Black liberation movement, a discussion is necessary on how the proposals of the Black Agenda and the decisions of the National Black Political Convention relate to mass actions and the fight for a Black party. This can help prevent the advanced ideas and sentiments of the Black community expressed in the Black Political Agenda and the National Black Political Convention from being used only as a figleaf for the Democratic Party politicking of Baraka, the Black Congressional Caucus, and other "spokespeople" for the Gary Black Convention and the Black liberation movement.

In addition to the weaknesses outlined above, the Agenda's list of demands contains notable omissions and inadequacies. For example, instead of demanding the immediate and unconditional withdrawal of all U.S. forces from Indochina, the Agenda calls for setting the date for withdrawal—the end of 1973!

The Agenda lacks a well-rounded series of demands related to the problems faced by Black workers. Only the demand for a minimum wage of $2.50 and support for Black unions parallel to existing unions that exclude Blacks are included. This is a weakness when it is considered that over 90 percent of the Black community are workers or unemployed.

Important additions should include: preferential hiring and promotion for Black workers, equal pay for Black workers, support to the right of all workers including public workers and teachers to organize unions. While the Black Agenda gives support to the idea of parallel Black unions where Black workers feel this is the only way to fight racism in the unions, the Agenda should also include support to Black caucuses in existing unions that have been formed to fight for the demands of Black workers.

While the Agenda's proposals for alleviating the conditions in the Black community run completely contrary to the "wage-freeze," and other aspects of Nixon's "New Economic Policy," the Agenda needs a program of demands to deal with the rising unemployment, inflation, and attacks on the right to organize spawned by Phase Two. An important demand along these lines would be the establishment of price-watching committees in the Black community to control rents and prices. Another demand would be a division of the hours of work among all who want jobs with no reduction in pay, plus a rise in all wages to match rises in the cost of living.

While the Black Political Agenda raises the demand for community controlled day-care centers, the Agenda contains none of the other demands raised by Black women in their struggle against their dual oppression—as women and as Black people. Demands for equal pay and equal access to job and educational opportunities for Black women should have been included.

Still another omission is a demand against the forced sterilizations many Black women face in white-controlled hospitals or as a result of welfare programs. Another demand in the fight for the right of Black women to control their own bodies is for a repeal of all laws against abortion, and for free abortions on demand in clinics controlled by the Black community. Black women suffer the most from the antiabortion laws—dying or being maimed by quack abortionists because, unlike many white women, they are not able to pay for expensive illegal abortions or trips to states or countries where abortions are legal. Part of the oppression of the Black community by American capitalism is that Black women lack control over their own bodies. Every Black mother should be a willing mother, every Black child a wanted child.

Still another weakness in the Agenda in relation to Black women is that it refers continually to Black people as the Black "man" or to our predecessors as "our fathers." These terms exclude the role of Black women both in our current oppression as an equal part of our people and in the heritage of revolutionary struggle of Afro-Americans.

Despite all these weaknesses, the Black Agenda, and the rise in Black political consciousness it signifies, gives signs of important opportunities for the entire Black struggle. While the words of the Agenda stop short of proclaiming the need for a Black political party and for a mass struggle for Black control of the Black community, the essence of the demands and the nationalist language of the Black Political Agenda are consistent with these two courses of action.

This can only help expose the bankruptcy of those who urge that the Black liberation struggle support the Democratic Party. More significantly, the prominence of the Black Agenda—passed by the most representative gathering of Black people in years—can give added confidence and legitimacy to those who fully support its demands. Moreover, faced with its current economic crisis, American capitalism is even less able to give itself a liberal face by granting minor concessions, setting up poverty programs and foundation grants, and using other means to buy off sections of the Black liberation movement.

The Black Agenda and the Black Political Convention, despite the wishes of some of their initiators, have brought a Black political party and a victory in the struggle for Black control of the Black community much closer.

SECTION IX. AFTER GARY

In the period following the 1972 Gary convention, the Black movement went through a number of important experiences and debates around the question of independent political action and whether or not to participate in or to support capitalist political parties.

This section begins with an excerpt from an article by Derrick Morrison that describes the actions of the Congressional Black Caucus in steering the movement for independent Black political action into the Democratic party following the Gary convention. In addition, this section includes a report from the National Black Assembly's 1974 congress in Little Rock, Arkansas; a polemic by Tony Thomas against the Communist Party's strategy for the Black struggle; a report on the 1976 NBA convention in Cincinnati; and in the final selection, some remarks by SWP National Secretary Jack Barnes on the status of independent Black political action following the 1978 elections. Barnes makes particular reference to the unsuccessful campaign by Charles Evers for U.S. Senate in Mississippi.

From Gary to Miami
by Derrick Morrison

At the National Black Political Convention in Gary the Black politicians there wound up committing themselves to the very radical and uncompromising National Black Political Agenda.

The Agenda was the major document that emerged from the convention. It indicted white capitalist society for the long list of social ills plaguing the national Black community. To resolve these ills the Agenda outlined a program on the theme of Black control of the Black community. This basic nationalist theme permeated the whole document

Although the idea of a Black party was implicit in the Agenda, the Black politicians moved to do the impossible—which was to take the Agenda from Gary to the Democratic Party national convention at Miami Beach.

In the eyes of the politicians, the Agenda was the mandate they had been given to act as national power brokers for Black interests at the Democratic

Reprinted from *International Socialist Review*, October 1972

Party convention. In exchange for Black support, they wanted one of the white presidential aspirants to commit himself to the Agenda. This commitment, of course, would involve nothing more than a campaign promise.

But the farther the Black politicians got from Gary and the closer they approached Miami Beach, the more it dawned on them that the Agenda would be too hot to hold for bargaining purposes at the Democratic convention.

Aside from the reaction to the Agenda by white presidential aspirants, these politicians had trouble uniting other Black politicians and Democratic officials around the Agenda.

So on June 1 the Congressional Black Caucus unveiled what they called the "Black Bill of Rights." This document was considerably milder than the Agenda. But to give it a militant touch, a couple of the Black congressmen declared that the twelve demands in the bill were "nonnegotiable." The Democratic convention would have to either take it or leave it. It was in this fashion that they chucked aside the Agenda.

But again, as these politicians edged closer and closer to Miami, the bill of rights too was jettisoned. It got lost in the shuffle as the Black politicians hurried to climb aboard the McGovern bandwagon.

In the end the politicians announced that three promises had been extracted from McGovern. McGovern, they said, promised to appoint more Blacks to the U.S. Supreme Court, to give 10 percent of all federal job patronage within the states to Blacks, and to shell out some money for voter registration in the Black communities.

McGovern didn't have to sign anything. And he was not present at the press conference where D. C. congressional delegate Walter Fauntroy announced the promises. The only time that McGovern appeared at a press conference with Fauntroy and other Black politicians was when they announced their support of him.

I suppose that if we look at the promises from the vantage point of the Black Democrats, they were great and magnanimous gestures. If another Black is appointed to the Supreme Court he will undoubtedly come from the ranks of the Black politicians and lawyers. If some federal patronage is handed out, this will help oil the machines that the Black Democrats are trying to construct. And if some more Blacks are added to the registration rolls, this will facilitate the election and reelection of more Black Democratic officeholders.

But if we look at these campaign promises from the vantage point of the Black masses, from the vantage point of the searing crisis and decay of the ghetto, then they become a cruel hoax. McGovern's promises, even if they are carried out, do not even begin to speak to the problems of the masses.

The peddling of Black votes to McGovern also reveals that the methods of the Black Democrats in no way measure up to the tasks at hand. Far-reaching and fundamental changes have to be brought about to resolve the social ills plaguing the national Black community. This was the point made by the Black Agenda. The retreat of the Black politicians from the Agenda registered in a new way the basic incompatibility of a program for Black control of the Black community and the Democratic and Republican parties. Any program or struggle for Black control runs up against and contradicts the rule of the Democratic and Republican parties.

This irreconcilable contradiction between the aspirations for Black control and the two capitalist parties is something that we have to patiently and painstakingly explain. The illusions on this score run very deep as we can see from the popularity the Congressional Black Caucus enjoys in the Black community. And the depth of the illusions are readily observable in the pro-Democratic Party strategy being pursued by those Black nationalists under the influence of Imamu Amiri Baraka and the Congress of African People (CAP).

Baraka basically sells his strategy on the contention that this is the way to influence the Black politicians, this is the way to begin to make the politicians responsible and accountable to the Black community.

And in his thinking if the nationalists are able to exert this influence their standing and prestige is bound to rise. In such a fashion, nationalism will become more legitimate and attractive in the eyes and minds of the Black community.

Need for Independent Party Raised at National Black Political Convention
by Norman Oliver

LITTLE ROCK, Ark.—Seventeen hundred Black people made the trip to Little Rock March 15–17 for the Second National Black Political Convention.

Uppermost in the minds of most convention delegates was the question of how Blacks could organize to deal with the racist oppression Black

Reprinted from the *Militant*, March 29, 1974

people suffer today. Many of the speeches to the gathering reflected anger and frustration at the fact that no solutions to the problems facing Black people have been forthcoming.

The point was made again and again that through organizing to gain political power, Black people could begin to deal with unemployment, rotten housing, racist education, and so on.

Unfortunately, a strategy did not emerge out of the convention that could lead toward gaining real political power for Black people. This was because the convention organizers and most of the delegates were oriented toward working through the two-party system.

In the main speeches—a number of which were given by Democratic Party politicians—and in most of the workshops, delegates were urged to work toward electing Black officials. It was assumed, though not always stated, that this could best be done through the Democratic Party.

Imamu Amiri Baraka, chairman of the Congress of African People, played a central leadership role in the convention. Baraka and the forces around him believe that Black people can make gains in the fight against racist oppression by working as a faction within the Democratic Party.

At the same time, there were forces at the convention who argued, correctly, that the Black struggle cannot be advanced by supporting the Democratic or Republican parties. They advocated that Black people break from these parties and create an independent Black political party.

A resolution calling for a Black party was submitted to the resolutions committee by the Georgia delegation. The resolution said in part:

> Such an independent party should not only provide an independent electoral pole for the Black community, but should also be rooted in independent mass struggles in the Black community.
>
> A Black party should build struggles against racist education and for community control of schools. It should support the strikes and struggles of Black workers. It should champion the demands and struggles of Black women.
>
> It should lead the fight against Watergate-style victimization and harassment of the Black Liberation Movement. It should fight police repression and fight for a police force drawn from the Black community. It should support solidarity actions with African Liberation Movements and with Black political prisoners.
>
> Such an independent party while struggling around this type of program should also fight for complete control of the Black community and lead the struggle for Black self-determination.
>
> We can only wage such a struggle by building a party totally independent of the Democratic and Republican party, by building a party that gives no support to any Democrat or Republican in elections, be he Black or white.

The Democratic Party supporters at the convention did everything they could to prevent a real discussion of this resolution. Maynard Jackson, mayor of Atlanta, put pressure on members of the Georgia delegation to withdraw it

By the end of the convention, Jackson had succeeded in having the resolution watered down by removing language calling for a complete break with the Democratic and Republican parties, while maintaining the call for a Black party.

The call for a break with the Democratic and Republican parties and for launching an independent party won the support of a number of delegates. The Wisconsin delegation, which included delegates from the Black Masses Party in Milwaukee, supported the original and later the amended resolution.

Other delegations that had presented resolutions calling for a Black party included New Jersey, Colorado, Pennsylvania, Maryland, and Massachusetts.

When amended the Georgia resolution finally came to the floor at the end of the convention, it was killed by a motion to table. In arguing to table it, Ron Daniels, a leader of the Ohio Black Assembly, asserted that he was for a Black party, but now was not the time to begin to build one.

Gary convention

By voting to table the resolution on the Black party and by orienting the conference to a discussion of how to organize to elect Black Democrats, the Little Rock convention continued along the same course followed since the Black Political Convention held in Gary, Ind., two years ago.

At Gary, some 8,000 Black people gathered to discuss how to win Black political power. The idea of an independent Black party was raised on the convention floor. But convention organizers prevented a full discussion of this question, and in the two years since Gary, the national and state Black Assemblies—composed of delegates to the Gary convention—have followed a consistent policy of supporting Democrats.

Overall, the Little Rock meeting was a step backward from Gary. There was less preconvention publicity, and fewer people were present.

At Gary a "Black Agenda" was drawn up outlining solutions to many of the problems facing Black people. Though stopping short of advocating a Black party, the Agenda pointed to the need for independent struggles.

At Little Rock, discussion of the Black Agenda and how to implement it was ruled out of order.

Workshops

In line with the view of those organizing the Little Rock meeting that the key task was to get people to work to elect Black Democrats, key convention workshops were devoted to the technical aspects of working in the Democratic Party. The workshops were not designed to evoke political discussion and were oriented to such topics as "Financing a campaign," led by Congressman John Conyers (D-Mich.), and "Party involvement," led by another Democratic politician.

The plenary discussion on resolutions was held on the last day of the convention. Only a few hours were scheduled for this discussion, and because it was put off until the end of the convention, many of the delegates had left for home before it began.

The final address was given by Owusu Sadaukai, who is the head of the North Carolina Black Assembly and a national leader of the African Liberation Support Committee.

Sadaukai pointed repeatedly to the need for a "Black fighting organization" and called for an all-out attack against racism, imperialism, and capitalism. But he stopped short of calling for a break from the two capitalist parties—the Republicans and Democrats—that are the main perpetrators of these evils.

Sadaukai called for support to the actions planned for the spring by the African Liberation Support Committee. One of the achievements of the convention was the adoption of a resolution proposed by the African Liberation Support Committee.

This resolution designated May as African Liberation Month and called for local demonstrations on May 19 and a national march on Washington, D.C., on May 26 in solidarity with the liberation struggles in southern Africa.

Only a handful of Black Democratic politicians came to Little Rock. The most prominent among these were Gary Mayor Richard Hatcher, Atlanta Mayor Maynard Jackson, and Congressman Ron Dellums.

One of the most conspicuous absences was that of Representative Charles Diggs Jr. (D-Mich.). Diggs announced the day the convention opened that he was dropping out of the National Black Assembly, of which he was cochairman.

Many of these officials felt they had been burned at the Gary convention because they could not go along with some of the radical proposals outlined in the Black Agenda. Because of their loyalty to the Democratic Party, they had also been made quite nervous by the fact that the idea of a Black party had been raised at Gary.

After the Gary convention, the Black Democrats and convention organizers such as Baraka dumped the Black Agenda and drafted in its place a more moderate Black "Bill of Rights," which they used to bargain with at the Democratic Party convention in 1972.

At Little Rock, there was no evaluation of what the Black Democrats had done in this regard, nor did the convention leadership initiate any discussion of the record of the Democratic Party in failing to deal with the problems of Black people.

Black political power

To overcome the present condition of political powerlessness of Black America, it is necessary to break from the political parties of the capitalist ruling class and build an independent Black party.

This was the all important question raised by the supporters of the Black party resolution at Little Rock, and this is the reality that the masses of Black people will come to grips with if real gains are to be made in the fight for Black liberation.

It is correct to seek the support of Black Democrats in the concrete struggles of Black people. For example, it is a good idea to get their endorsement for the African Liberation Day demonstrations. But this is totally different from the "unity without uniformity" advocated by the organizers of the Little Rock convention. Their "unity" is predicated on support to the Democratic Party, and that is a dead end for the Black community.

Many convention speakers harshly criticized the Black elected officials who failed to attend.

Some were not present because they were afraid of being associated with a gathering they felt they might not be able to completely control.

Black Power: How It Will Be Won
by Tony Thomas

The title for Henry Winston's book, *Strategy for a Black Agenda*, is based on the "National Black Political Agenda," adopted at a Black political convention held in Gary, Ind., in 1972.

The Gary Black Agenda, accepted by most of the 8,000 Black delegates and observers who attended the convention, was a radical statement of aims and demands. It spoke of the social crisis facing Black people, blamed these conditions on "a society built on the twin foundations of white racism and white capitalism," and called for "fundamental change."

The Agenda denounced the "betrayal" of Black people by the Democrats and Republicans and called for "an independent Black political movement" to struggle for Black control of the Black community.

Though not the intention of the Democratic Party-oriented organizers of the Gary meeting, the logic of the Black Agenda was to move to construct an independent Black party that could mobilize the masses of Afro-Americans in uncompromising struggle against the capitalist status quo. This radical logic of the Agenda proved to be quite an embarrassment to Charles Diggs, Richard Hatcher, and Imamu Baraka—the key convention organizers—and it was soon shelved.

At the recent Black political convention in Little Rock further discussion on the Gary Agenda was ruled out of order.

Winston, national chairman of the Communist Party, appropriates the term "Black Agenda" for his book without explaining the content of the original document. And he lays out a "strategy" that runs counter to the independent thrust implicit in the Gary Agenda.

Winston falsely claims that his book is a revolutionary Marxist treatment of the Black struggle. But an examination of what he writes, and a look at the theory and practice of his party, shows that his view is nonrevolutionary and non-Marxist.

In order to cover up the Communist Party's reformist record, Winston has to falsify the history of the Black liberation movement. The most telling example of this is his examination of the dispute that broke out in the mid-1960s between the supporters of Martin Luther King and the advocates of Black power in the Student Nonviolent Coordinating Committee (SNCC).

During the struggles of the 1960s, the Communist Party was a consistent supporter of the policies of Martin Luther King, as against the more militant stance of such figures as Malcolm X, and later, Stokely Carmichael and other Black Power advocates. Winston's *Black Agenda* attempts to justify this approach.

Winston has nothing but praise for King. He writes, "Though not a Marxist, King was steadily moving toward a strategy that tended to coincide with the Marxist-Leninist concept of an antimonopoly policy. . . ."

In contrast, Winston claims that beginning around 1965 Black radicals such as Stokely Carmichael, James Forman, and others, "began to

Reprinted from the *Militant*, April 12, 1974

step up their attacks on the Civil Rights struggle. *They placed themselves in opposition to King, who was determined not to abandon, but to strengthen, the forces of the Civil Rights Decade, to deepen and broaden them into a realignment that could carry the struggle against poverty and racist oppression to a new level."* (Emphasis in original.)

Winston suggests that the major point of controversy between Black Power supporters and King was whether Blacks should ally with other working-class forces. He gives the impression that in this debate King proposed a "working class" strategy while Carmichael and others proposed a divisive nationalist policy that "helped monopoly" by opposing a class-struggle orientation.

This is a distortion on all counts. The real issue at stake in the dispute over Black Power was whether or not the Black movement was to continue to be subordinated to the liberal wing of the Democratic Party and the forces aligned to it.

King was for keeping the movement tied to the Democratic liberals. Carmichael and other Black Power advocates were beginning to question or to oppose support to the Democratic Party. In Alabama in 1966, SNCC helped build the Lowndes County Freedom Organization, an independent Black political party, while King supported Richmond Flowers, Democratic candidate for governor.

King was an ideological pacifist, who opposed self-defense of Blacks facing racist attacks, while supporters of Black Power defended this right.

SNCC, one of the main activist organizations of the southern civil rights struggles, grew out of the lunch-counter sit-ins organized by Black students in 1960. For years, SNCC played a key role in organizing the struggles for voting rights and other democratic rights of Afro-Americans.

The move toward Black Power came when SNCC activists learned through their own experience in struggle that they could not rely on Democratic Party politicians or white liberals to eradicate racism. The Black Power slogan expressed the idea that it was only through taking their destiny into their own hands that Black people could make gains. It was a recognition that the liberal politicians could not be trusted, that they would sell out the struggle.

Support for Black Power did not presuppose a rejection of alliances with working-class whites. It was an expression of the feeling that Blacks should not have to wait for the radicalization of white workers before launching an independent struggle.

Far from being an isolated trend, as Winston implies, the call for Black Power met with a favorable response in Black communities throughout the country. Millions of Afro-Americans were inspired by the concept that Black people should develop the political power to take control over their political, economic, and social destinies.

The new Black consciousness was expressed in the rebellions that exploded in Detroit, Newark, and other cities. It was also expressed in the growth of support among Black people for the freedom struggles in the colonial world, in the explosion of struggles by Black high school and college students, and in the increased militancy and organization by Black workers in the plants.

The surge of Black pride and militancy that came on the heels of the spread of the nationalist ideas of Malcolm X is not even acknowledged by Winston as being a significant factor in bringing about the gains won in the 1960s. Instead, Winston has almost nothing but criticism for the Black nationalist tendencies, and all praise is given to the currents represented by King and others who resisted the nationalist radicalization.

Of course, King and the Southern Christian Leadership Conference (SCLC), the organization he led, did make a contribution to the battles of the 1960s. SCLC did, on specific occasions, initiate actions involving masses of Black people. But King and his supporters generally played a moderating role, trying to keep the struggle within limits acceptable to SCLC's white liberal benefactors.

When Malcolm X opposed both the Democratic and Republican candidates in the 1964 elections, Martin Luther King supported Lyndon Johnson (as did the Communist Party). King even joined with other Black leaders to call a moratorium on Black protests in the period before the elections in order to enhance Johnson's chances.

King always saw the mobilization of working people in struggle only as a means of pressuring the capitalist politicians, never as a means for creating, step by step, an alternative to capitalist rule. His outlook was limited to reforming the capitalist status quo, while Malcolm X, and later many Black

Power advocates, saw the need for revolutionary change.

In posing the need to break the capitalist stranglehold over the politics of the Black community, the supporters of Black Power were the ones responsible for taking the movement to "a new level." They were attempting to advance the struggle without subordinating it to the needs of the "liberal" exploiters. Thus it was this trend that came closer to representing the real need for Afro-Americans—and white workers as well—to move to the direction of building a class-struggle leadership in the fight against oppression.

To rationalize the CP's opposition to the militant nationalist currents of the 1960s, Winston preys upon the fact that many of the nationalist youth ended up going in an ultraleft direction.

The most important example of this problem was the Black Panther Party, which reached its height in late 1968 and early 1969. The Panthers spread on the basis of being a national Black political organization that supported Black control of the Black community and opposed the Democratic and Republican parties.

The Panthers went off on an ultra-left tangent, substituting rhetoric based on their own recognition of the need for revolution for a program that could lead the masses of Blacks to hold such consciousness. Their "pick up the gun" rhetoric and their abstention from the real struggles taking place made it impossible for them to build an effective mass movement, and made them vulnerable to government attack.

Winston's criticisms of the Panthers are not based on the need to build a mass movement independent of the capitalist parties. He derides the Panthers' ultraleft errors, but fails to criticize their opportunist errors, most importantly, their turn toward the Democratic Party.

Winston implies that the only alternative to the ultraleft policies of the Panthers is the reformism of such figures as King. Purposely ignored by him is the revolutionary strategy of building a mass movement that is politically independent of the ruling class and its parties.

It is thus not surprising that almost no space in Winston's book is devoted to Malcolm X, the Black revolutionary figure of the 1960s who contributed most to outlining a strategy that could avoid ultraleftism and reformism.

The concept put forward by Winston as the solution to the problems faced by the movement is that of the "anti-monopoly coalition." The closest Winston gets to defining this concept is to say that the "anti-monopoly coalition" is a bloc "involving the Black and white sectors of the working class, the Black liberation movement, the Puerto Rican and Chicano masses, and all others opposed to war and poverty."

Since the term anti-monopoly coalition is never more concretely defined than this, it is difficult to understand simply by reading Winston's book what he and the Communist Party think supporters of Afro-American liberation and socialism should do.

It is only by looking at other Communist Party sources, and at what the CP is doing *in practice*, that one discovers what the "anti-monopoly coalition" really is.

In an article in the July 1972 issue of *Political Affairs*, "Theoretical Journal of the Communist Party," William Weinstone, a longtime CP leader, gives this description of "the nature of an anti-monopoly coalition":

> It is an agreement in one form or another of various working-class and democratic-minded organizations and people—workers, farmers, professionals, intellectuals, youth, women, students, some sections of *small and medium businessmen and others*. It consists of people of various political views—Republican, Democratic, independent, Socialist, Communist and others. (Emphasis added.)

If by this the CP meant attempting to win over Black people and others who vote for Democrats or Republicans to struggles against racial and class oppression, this would be one thing. But, the practice of the CP shows that this is not what the "anti-monopoly coalition" means. It means winning over Black and white working people to support liberal Democratic (and sometimes Republican) politicians. This strategy is to culminate one day in the distant future in an "anti-monopoly" party, a third, "progressive," capitalist party.

One of the most recent examples of the CP's anti-monopoly coalition strategy was their support last fall for Coleman Young, who was elected on the Democratic Party ticket as mayor of Detroit. The CP's *Daily World* hailed Young's victory as an example of "independent political action."

Young's election was significant in that he is the first Black mayor of Detroit, and his election showed the potential power of the Black vote. Nevertheless, his candidacy was not "independent" of the capitalist parties. Young was supported by some of the biggest capitalists in Detroit. They favored his election as a way of nourishing the illusion among Detroit Blacks that something would be done about their conditions of life.

The CP is well aware of the coalition between Young and Detroit monopolists. James Jackson, national educational director of the CP, makes this explicit in the March 2 *Daily World* when he writes:

> For the successful realization of a program for civic improvements and to make gains in the fight to provide jobs for the unemployed and economic input for a revival of business activity, the administration of Mayor Young must have the cooperation of important sections of the industrialists. Such big capitalists as Henry Ford have their own need for the development of Detroit; they are coming from far different positions than Mayor Young and are motivated by the pursuit of their own special interests. The broadest alignment of class forces are both possible and necessary for addressing the problems of urban crisis which holds Detroit in its grip as it does scores of other cities of the country.

Thus, the CP spreads the illusion that through the Democratic Party, and through an alliance with "progressive" capitalists, the conditions of Black people can be changed. *The so-called anti-monopoly coalition includes the monopolists themselves!*

It's worth noting, if only in passing, that this same strategy—dressed up as "the peaceful road to socialism"—paved the way for the recent tragic defeat for the workers movement in Chile. There, it meant supporting the capitalist government of Allende and relying on the "democratic" capitalist army to combat the right-wing opponents of reforms being won by working people.

Experience after experience of the Black community—including the experience of electing Black Democratic Party mayors—shows that support to the Democratic and Republican parties has not led to the alleviation of the problems of the masses of people. These parties are dominated by the capitalist rulers, who profit from racial oppression and class exploitation.

A real working-class strategy is one that seeks to build a mass revolutionary workers party that can lead the struggles of working people and all the oppressed with the goal of taking power out of the hands of the capitalists.

Any break by working people with the two capitalist parties, such as the development of a mass Black party or a labor party based on the trade unions, would be a step in this direction. A Black party would also be an effective vehicle for winning immediate concessions from the capitalist government, and it would provide an example of workers' political self-reliance for Black and white workers alike. The development of a mass Black party would so weaken the Democratic Party that the labor movement would be compelled to reconsider its reliance on the Democratic Party and take the road of independent political action.

But the Communist Party calls neither for the creation of a Black party nor a labor party. They have been hostile to any trends within the Black and labor movements that move in this direction, just as they have opposed the development of the fledgling independent Chicano parties—the Raza Unida parties—in the Southwest.

Rather than posing a class-struggle strategy based on organizing the working class and its allies independent of their exploiters, the "anti-monopoly coalition" strategy of the Communist Party counsels collaboration with these exploiters.

Winston's book is nothing but a rationalization and cover-up of this non-revolutionary strategy.

Black Convention Debates Electoral Action
by Baxter Smith

CINCINNATI—The three-day National Black Political Convention came to an end March 20 when U.S. Rep. Ronald Dellums, in the face of a strong desire by participants to launch an independent campaign, declined the group's presidential nomination.

"I am unequivocal in my desire not to run. This is not my role and not my moment," the California Democrat told the 888 delegates and observers.

Dellums's remarks came at the third biennial national Black convention, hosted by the National Black Political Assembly (NBA).

The first convention, in Gary, Indiana, in 1972, drew 8,000 participants. The assembly was founded after Gary to implement the measures embodied in the militant Black Agenda that the convention adopted. It also played host to the Little Rock, Arkansas, Black convention in 1974 that drew 1,700 people.

Eager anticipation

Most conventioners appeared to be students and working people between the ages of twenty and thirty. Some heads of community agencies were present, as well as a small number of prominent Black intellectuals and professors. Unlike previous conventions, however, there were very few Black elected officials.

From the enthusiasm and anticipation displayed at the nominating rally, there was little doubt that people had come with the intention of drawing up a platform speaking to the urgent concerns of the Black community. Most of all they were looking forward to taking the bold step of launching an independent presidential campaign to challenge the decades-old racist rule of the Democratic and Republican parties.

The news media—given the widespread disaffection among Blacks over the inability of the system to meet Black needs, and given the potential of an independent Black presidential campaign as a focus for that disaffection—gave prominent notice to the gathering before it occurred. There were also major network and newspaper coverage and analysis during the convention and upon its conclusion.

In January leaders of the Black Assembly had announced their intention to draft State Sen. Julian Bond, a Georgia Democrat. Bond said he was "pleased and flattered," but would announce his decision at a future date.

The day before the opening of the convention, Bond went on national radio and announced that he was turning down the assembly's offer, labeling the idea premature.

"Black voters are unprepared to support an independent candidacy," he asserted.

After Bond refused, assembly leaders announced their intention to try to draft Dellums.

Ron Daniels, assembly chairperson, and Mtangulizi Sanyika, who holds the post of "chairperson of political development," told the delegates that in previous discussions Dellums had placed a number of conditions on any decision to run.

Dellums's conditions

First, Dellums had indicated that he had to be free to attend the July convention of the Democratic party where, he said, he would be agitating and heightening the party's "contradictions." Then, if the Democrats did not nominate someone to his liking, he might consider running as the NBA candidate. Even after the Democratic convention, if Dellums decided to run, it was explained, he would impose other conditions he would detail at that time.

Sanyika also described the National Committee for Peoples Politics (NCPP), a group set up to be the campaign organization for the assembly's presidential ticket.

The formal makeup of the NCPP, it was explained, is 51 percent Black and 49 percent white, Puerto Rican, Chicano, Native American, and Asian-American.

The NCPP is supposed to nominate a vice-presidential candidate and exercise decision-making

Reprinted from the *Militant*, April 9, 1976

power over aspects of the campaign. Some of the forces associated with the NCPP, however, favor the strategy of pressuring the Democratic party for concessions. Others favor the creation of something like the 1968 Peace and Freedom party, which ran Eldridge Cleaver for president. This sort of party is set up to protest certain evils of capitalism without getting rid of it.

None of this was explained to the delegates and it was simply stated that it is necessary to have input from other nationalities and races because any presidential campaign would have the potential of appealing to them.

The following day suspicions and sentiment opposing some aspects of what had been proposed were expressed during the plenary session.

Some were confused about what role whites would have in the campaign under the proposal.

Robb Wright, a New York delegate and member of the Socialist Workers party, explained that the campaign should be based on the Black community and have an independent thrust. He said it should point in the direction of a Black party. His remarks won applause.

Nonetheless, a proposal to approve the NCPP was adopted.

Platform
Later that evening the platform was read to the delegates.

Some parts of it seem to dovetail with the militantly worded Black Agenda passed at Gary. There is a section favoring home rule for majority-Black Washington, D. C. Illegal surveillance and harassment by the CIA, FBI, and other government spy agencies were condemned. A proposal calling for "nationalization of all our means of production" was adopted. Delegates voted to oppose racist redlining practices in housing.

In a section on education the platform reaffirms the right of Blacks to go to any school, but adds that the "highest priority should be on Black education in the Black community." The section also says that if Blacks are to be bused outside of the Black community, then it should be "to superior schools only."

The education section generally represents an advance over what was adopted at Gary, where all busing was condemned.

Other aspects of the platform, however, are not sufficient to cope with the urgent problems Blacks face. Although a plank was adopted favoring full employment, the platform never spells out what measures would have to be taken to bring it about, such as abolishing the war budget. There was no plank opposing the racist cutbacks in social services, which have affected Blacks the hardest.

Women's rights were not mentioned in the platform. However, a resolution urging passage of the Equal Rights Amendment and urging Black participation in the May 16 Springfield, Illinois, demonstration backing the ERA was adopted in the Black women's workshop.

Although workshop resolutions were supposed to be presented to the delegates for their approval, this was never done because of the tight schedule. One of the resolutions adopted in the workshops supported the April 24 national march on Boston for school desegregation. Another called for support to the case of J. B. Johnson, a Black frame-up victim in St Louis.

The climax of the convention came on Saturday night at the nominating rally.

Black people, Dellums said after a tumultuous introduction, "are being ground up like glass in the insanity of the system.

"I have never believed in blind allegiance to the Democratic party. But while others are out there posing the independent alternative, I had to be inside crystallizing the contradictions," he continued. "Therefore, I am not your candidate."

Understandably, there was considerable letdown, frustration, and alarm in the crowd after Dellums said no. This was indicative of the overwhelming desire to launch an independent Black presidential campaign.

The time for such a campaign is ripe. It would be a goodly step forward for the entire Black community, but only if the thrust of the campaign were clearly independent of the capitalist parties—educating people that the Democratic and Republican parties are among the biggest obstacles to any Black progress, and working to totally erase the support those parties enjoy in the Black community.

It is not at all clear that this is what the leadership of the assembly wants to do.

More and more, in public remarks, Daniels has

been pointing to the example of George Wallace and how he has been able to pressure the Democratic party.

"George Wallace has never come close to winning the presidency, and never expected to," says Daniels. "But his presence in national politics over the last eight or ten years has driven both parties drastically to the right. Blacks could become this same kind of force to drive both parties to the left."

The gathering here this weekend raised crucial questions for Black people. At the convention there was overwhelming disgust with the Democratic and Republican parties, which are both ignoring the needs of Blacks.

What should be the relationship of Black people to the Democratic party? What would an independent Black political campaign do? How should it relate to the allies of Black people and the working class as a whole? How should it relate to radical groups?

These and other questions will be examined in future issues of the *Militant*.

Working-class Politics and Capitalist Politics
by Jack Barnes

The 1978 elections registered some significant setbacks for independent Black and Chicano political action. This continues a trend that has been going on for some time.

In Mississippi, Charles Evers—the brother of the assassinated 1960s civil rights leader Medgar Evers—campaigned against the nominees of the Democratic and Republican parties. But it is wrong to refer to his campaign as an independent campaign or to say that this campaign represented a break with the twin capitalist parties that perpetuate racism. The evidence is to the contrary.

It is not enough just to note that Evers did not run as either a Democrat or Republican. Because the political content of his campaign was in no way a break from capitalist politics. Nor did it represent, even in a distorted or partial way, the interests of oppressed Blacks or the working class in Mississippi. Evers attacked busing, lambasted "welfare cheats," and came out in support of "right to work" laws and prayers in public schools. We don't know all his positions. But we don't need to know anything more.

Far from being a campaign that expressed the interests of Blacks or other working people in Mississippi, this campaign was an obstacle to charting a political course that could organize the working people of Mississippi to stand up to the employers' austerity offensive and ideological pressure.

Of course, many Black people voted for him despite these reactionary stands. But that doesn't change the character of his campaign. It simply points to the fact that faced with a choice between a Black and a white candidate, neither of whom has a clear program to advance the class struggle most members of the oppressed nationalities who vote will vote to increase the number of Blacks in public office and hope for the best.

But from all capitalist politicians we'll all get the worst.

Evers's sizable vote doesn't show any motion toward independent Black political action. What the Evers campaign does show is something quite different. It reveals the decisiveness of program on the electoral front. Independence is a programmatic question, that is, a class question. Of course, in some cases this can be largely implicit to begin with. The Freedom Now Party that developed in Michigan in 1964 didn't have a full-blown program for the transformation of society, although the program it did have was in the interests of Blacks and all workers. The decisive thing was the direction of motion. We supported the FNP as a working-class break from the capitalist parties by a segment of the oppressed Black population.

But as the pressure mounts to break out of the

Reprinted from *Party Organizer*, Vol. 3, No. 1, March 1979

framework of capitalist politics, the rulers are going to make more and more of an effort to come up with safety valves that keep the exploited and oppressed stuck in lesser-evilism. If necessary, they will increase the number of Black candidates running. They will find this woman to run, that young person, this "populist," that gay person, this "environmentalist." They will even start running some "socialist" Democrats. Just as long as they don't break out of the framework of capitalist politics, but instead serve as a way of sucking people back in.

That is how the capitalist press used the Evers campaign. It was used consciously throughout the South to bolster the rulers' propaganda about the need to cut social expenditures by eliminating busing, that is, to roll back desegregation; to pass right-to-work laws so there can be "freedom of choice"; and to make other reactionary moves. All of this was strengthened by the Evers campaign, which the southern bourgeois press said proved "all the people" wanted restriction on "out-of-control social spending."

EXPAND YOUR REVOLUTIONARY LIBRARY

Lenin's Final Fight
Speeches and Writings, 1922–23
V.I. LENIN

In 1922 and 1923, V.I. Lenin, central leader of the world's first socialist revolution, waged what was to be his last political battle—one that was lost following his death. At stake was whether that revolution, and the international communist movement it led, would remain on the revolutionary proletarian course that brought workers and peasants to power in October 1917. $17. Also in Spanish, Farsi, and Greek.

Maurice Bishop Speaks
The Grenada Revolution and Its Overthrow, 1979–83

The triumph of the 1979 revolution in the Caribbean island of Grenada under the leadership of Maurice Bishop gave hope to millions throughout the Americas. Invaluable lessons from the workers and farmers government destroyed by a Stalinist-led counterrevolution in 1983. $20

In Defense of the US Working Class
MARY-ALICE WATERS

Drawing on the fighting traditions of the oppressed and exploited of all colors and national origins, in 2018 tens of thousands of teachers and other working people in West Virginia, Oklahoma, and other states waged victorious strikes. They fought for dignity and respect for themselves, their families, and for all working people. $7. Also in Spanish, French, Farsi, and Greek.

50 Years of Covert Operations in the US
Washington's Political Police and the American Working Class
LARRY SEIGLE, FARRELL DOBBS, STEVE CLARK

How class-conscious workers have fought against the drive to build the "national security" state essential to maintaining capitalist rule. $10. Also in Spanish and Farsi.

The Clintons' Anti-Working-Class Record
Why Washington Fears Working People
JACK BARNES

What working people need to know about the profit-driven course of Democrats and Republicans alike over the last three decades. And the political awakening of workers seeking to understand and resist the capitalist rulers' assaults. $10. Also in Spanish, French, Farsi, and Greek.

Malcolm X Talks to Young People

"The young generation of whites, Blacks, browns, whatever else—you're living at a time of revolution," said Malcolm in 1964. "And I for one will join with anyone, I don't care what color you are, as long as you want to change this miserable condition that exists on this earth." Four talks and an interview in the last months of Malcolm's life. $12. Also in Spanish, French, Farsi, and Greek.

Pathfinder Press accessible e-books for the blind, those with low vision, or other challenges reading print books

For a list of current accessible titles, go to: pathfinderpress.com/collections/books-for-the-blind.

Visit bookshare.org for information on how to sign up.

PATHFINDERPRESS.COM

ALSO FROM PATHFINDER

Labor, Nature, and the Evolution of Humanity
The Long View of History
FREDERICK ENGELS, KARL MARX
GEORGE NOVACK
MARY-ALICE WATERS

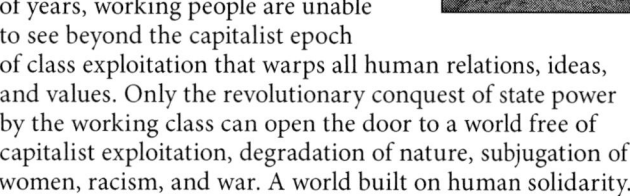

Without understanding that social labor, transforming nature, has driven humanity's evolution for millions of years, working people are unable to see beyond the capitalist epoch of class exploitation that warps all human relations, ideas, and values. Only the revolutionary conquest of state power by the working class can open the door to a world free of capitalist exploitation, degradation of nature, subjugation of women, racism, and war. A world built on human solidarity. A socialist world. $12. Also in Spanish and French.

Thomas Sankara Speaks
The Burkina Faso Revolution, 1983–87

Under Sankara's guidance, Burkina Faso's revolutionary government led peasants, workers, women, and youth to expand literacy; to sink wells, plant trees, erect housing; to combat women's oppression; to carry out land reform; to join others worldwide to free themselves from the imperialist yoke. $20. Also in French.

Women's Liberation and the African Freedom Struggle
THOMAS SANKARA

"There is no true social revolution without the liberation of women," explains the leader of the 1983–87 revolution in the West African country of Burkina Faso. $5. Also in Spanish, French, and Farsi.

U.S. Imperialism Has Lost the Cold War
JACK BARNES

The collapse of regimes across Eastern Europe and the USSR claiming to be communist did not mean workers and farmers there had been crushed. In today's sharpening capitalist conflicts and wars, these toilers are joining working people the world over in the class struggle against exploitation. In *New International* no. 11. $14. Also in Spanish, French, Farsi, and Greek.

By Any Means Necessary
MALCOLM X

"The imperialists know the only way you will voluntarily turn to the fox is to show you a wolf." In eleven speeches and interviews, Malcolm X presents a revolutionary alternative to this reformist trap, taking up political alliances, women's rights, US intervention in the Congo and Vietnam, capitalism and socialism, and more. $15

The Revolution Betrayed
What Is the Soviet Union and Where Is It Going?
LEON TROTSKY

In 1917 workers and peasants of Russia were the motor force for one of the deepest revolutions in history. Yet within ten years a political counterrevolution by a privileged social layer, whose chief spokesperson was Joseph Stalin, was being consolidated. The classic study of the Soviet workers state and its degeneration. $17. Also in Spanish, Farsi, and Greek.

Dynamics of the Cuban Revolution
A Marxist Appreciation
JOSEPH HANSEN

How did the Cuban Revolution unfold? Why is it an "unbearable challenge" to US imperialism? Why are its lessons important to working people everywhere?

In "Cuba—The acid test: A reply to ultraleft sectarians," one of more than 20 articles here, Hansen starts with facts—not doctrine pretending to be theory—to examine the class struggle unfolding in Cuba in the 1960s. He refutes the political blindness of leftists who denied the dialectical richness of the socialist revolution and communist leadership developing before their eyes. $23

Leon Trotsky on France

An assessment of the social and economic crisis that shook France in the mid-1930s in the aftermath of Hitler's rise to power in Germany, and a program to unite the working class and exploited peasantry to confront it. $17

The Low Point of Labor Resistance Is Behind Us
The Socialist Workers Party Looks Forward
JACK BARNES, MARY-ALICE WATERS, STEVE CLARK

The global order imposed by victors of the inter-imperialist slaughter of World War II is shattering, with explosive ramifications for workers and farmers worldwide. A long retreat by the working class and unions has come to an end. More and more workers of all ages, skin colors, and both sexes are saying, "Enough is enough!" This book highlights opportunities ahead for class-conscious workers to forge a labor party built on the unions. And a mass proletarian vanguard able to lead the struggle to end capitalist rule, opening a future for humanity. $10. Also in Spanish and French.

The History of the Russian Revolution
LEON TROTSKY

How, under Lenin's leadership, the Bolshevik Party led millions of workers and farmers to overthrow the state power of the landlords and capitalists in 1917 and bring to power a government that advanced their class interests at home and worldwide. Unabridged, 3 vols. in one. Written by one of the central leaders of that socialist revolution. $30. Also in French and Russian.

Teamster Rebellion
FARRELL DOBBS

The 1934 strikes that won union recognition for truckers and warehouse workers in Minneapolis and helped pave the way for the working-class social movement that built the industrial unions. The first of four volumes by a central leader of these battles. $16. Also in Spanish, French, Farsi, and Greek.

Democracy and Revolution
GEORGE NOVACK

The limitations and advances of various forms of democracy in class society, from its roots in ancient Greece through its rise and decline under capitalism. Discusses the emergence of Bonapartism, military dictatorship, and fascism, and how democracy will be advanced under a workers and farmers regime. $17

The Second Assassination of Maurice Bishop
STEVE CLARK

The lead article in *New International* no. 6 reviews the accomplishments of the 1979–83 revolution in the Caribbean island of Grenada. Explains the roots of the 1983 coup that led to the murder of revolutionary leader Maurice Bishop, and to the destruction of the workers and farmers government by a Stalinist political faction within the governing New Jewel Movement. $14 Also in Spanish and French.

The Fight against Fascism in the USA
Forty Years of Struggle Described by Participants
JAMES P. CANNON AND OTHERS

In 1939 some 50,000 people in New York City responded to a call by the Socialist Workers Party to answer a pro-Nazi rally of 20,000. "The question of how to fight fascism was answered in thunderous tones by the magnificent demonstration which raised the cry: Workers Defense Guards to crush the fascist danger!" $5

Are They Rich Because They're Smart?
Class, Privilege, and Learning under Capitalism
JACK BARNES

Exposes growing class inequalities in the US and the self-serving rationalizations of well-paid professionals who think their "brilliance" equips them to "regulate" working people, who don't know what's in our own best interest. $10. Also in Spanish, French, Farsi, and Arabic.

Capitalism and the Transformation of Africa
Reports from Equatorial Guinea
MARY-ALICE WATERS, MARTÍN KOPPEL

Describes how, as Equatorial Guinea is pulled into the world market, both a capitalist class and a working class are being born. Also documents the work of volunteer Cuban healthcare workers there—an expression of the living example of Cuba's socialist revolution. $10. Also in Spanish and Farsi.

PATHFINDERPRESS.COM

BUILDING A PROLETARIAN PARTY

In Defense of Marxism
Against the Petty-Bourgeois Opposition in the Socialist Workers Party
LEON TROTSKY

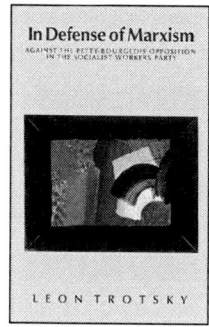

A reply to those in the revolutionary workers movement in the late 1930s bending to bourgeois patriotism during Washington's buildup to enter World War II. Trotsky explains why only a party fighting to bring workers into its ranks and leadership can steer a communist course. In the process, he defends the materialist and dialectical foundations of Marxism. $17. Also in Spanish.

The Struggle for a Proletarian Party
JAMES P. CANNON

"The workers of America have power enough to topple the structure of capitalism at home and to lift the whole world with them when they rise," Cannon asserts. On the eve of World War II, a founder of the communist movement in the US and leader of the Communist International in Lenin's time defends the program and party-building norms of Bolshevism. $20. Also in Spanish and Farsi.

Revolutionary Continuity
Marxist Leadership in the U.S.
The Early Years, 1848–1917
Birth of the Communist Movement, 1918–1922
FARRELL DOBBS

"Successive generations of proletarian revolutionists have participated in the movements of the working class and its allies.... Marxists today owe them not only homage for their deeds. We also have a duty to learn what they did wrong as well as right so their errors are not repeated." —*Farrell Dobbs*. Two volumes, $17 each.

The History of American Trotskyism, 1928–38
Report of a Participant
JAMES P. CANNON
$17. Also in Spanish and French.

The Transitional Program for Socialist Revolution
LEON TROTSKY

The Socialist Workers Party program, drafted by Trotsky in 1938, still guides the SWP and communists the world over. The party "uncompromisingly gives battle to all political groupings tied to the apron strings of the bourgeoisie. Its task—the abolition of capitalism's domination. Its aim—socialism. Its method—the proletarian revolution." $17. Also in Farsi.

Socialism on Trial
Testimony at Minneapolis Sedition Trial
JAMES P. CANNON

The revolutionary program of the working class, presented in response to frame-up charges of "seditious conspiracy" in 1941, on the eve of US entry into World War II. The defendants were leaders of the Minneapolis labor movement and the Socialist Workers Party. $15. Also in Spanish, French, and Farsi.

Their Trotsky and Ours
JACK BARNES

To lead the working class in a successful revolution, a mass proletarian party is needed whose cadres, well beforehand, have absorbed a world communist program, are proletarian in life and work, derive deep satisfaction from doing politics, and have forged a leadership with an acute sense of what to do next. This book is about building such a party. $12. Also in Spanish, French, and Farsi.

What Is to Be Done?
V.I. LENIN

The stakes in creating a disciplined organization of working-class revolutionaries capable of acting as a "tribune of the people, able to react to every manifestation of tyranny and oppression, no matter where it appears, to clarify for all and everyone the world-historic significance of the struggle for the emancipation of the proletariat." Written in 1902. $20

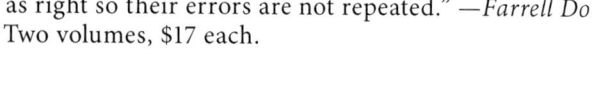